Eden, Indeed

Eden, Indeed

TALES, TRUTHS AND FABRICATIONS OF A SMALL TOWN BOY

Dave Delgardo

CHURCH OF THE OPEN ROAD PRESS

*Visit www.churchoftheopenroad.com
for further writings by Dave*

© 2023 David Delgardo. All rights reserved.

ISBN 978-1-952932-11-3

Produced by **Personal History Productions LLC**
Helping individuals and organizations record and preserve their histories as a legacy to last a lifetime and beyond
www.personalhistoryproductions.com
707.888.3446

This collection is dedicated to my grandchildren and theirs . . .
      and theirs . . .
           and theirs . . . with this hope:

That your growings-up be filled with adventure and mystery, wonder and folly, community and love . . .

    . . . and that those growings-up will continue for a lifetime.

Contents

Prelude   1

1   Charlie and Rex   4
2   Oranges, Peppermint Sticks and Coca-Cola   7
3   The Great Horseapple Wars of the Late 1950s   14
4   Playing Hooky from God   20
5   One New Year's Eve   29
6   At the Livestock Auction   32
7   Rope Swing   39
8   My First Two-Wheeler   43
9   Paxton Hotel   48
10 Bonfire of the Eight Year Olds   55
11 Sugar Blues   60
12 Nilley's Bomb Shelter   64
13 Mom's Manzanita Tea   71

14 The Day My Teacher Cried   76
15 Honey Run Bridge   81
16 Chesterfield Straights   91
17 The Art of Racing in November   98
18 Crossing Paths with Edward Abbey   101
19 A Final Voyage   108
20 Incident at the Jolly Kone   119
21 The First Grand Motorcycle Adventure   122
22 Blessed are the Meek   131
23 Roommate   140
24 Leon   151
25 My Run-in with Elmer   159
26 October Visitor   165
27 A Road Trip with Dad   172
28 Gathering Sticks for the Fire   186
29 Felling the Yule Tree   204
30 Mom's Holiday Rolls   206
31 "What Is the Greatest Gift?"   210

Postscript   215
Acknowledgments   219
About the Author   222

Prelude *1956*

SOUTHERN CALIFORNIA'S POST-WAR BOOM WAS GETTING to Dad. Barstow-based desert rat by upbringing, the congestion, the crowding, the smog, the living cheek-by-jowl in the suburbs of Los Angeles was simply not natural to him. It wasn't right. He needed elbowroom. He needed clear skies and fresh air. He needed mountains or deserts or pasturelands or orchards. He needed something—anything—other than sprawl. To Mom, a native of Houston and a child of a 1930s poor house, the tidy home they'd purchased on Colman Street in Altadena just after Beebo was born was as much as she dared dream for.

Barely past toddling at the time, I certainly have no recollections of the conversations that must have led up to his departure, but in 1957, Dad quit his job as a letter carrier, boarded a northbound Continental Trailways bus and somehow wound up in Chico. Perhaps that's as far as his ticket would carry him.

2   Prelude

Altadena House

There, he rented a room from a dowager, looked for work and tried to live on less than a dollar a day. He eventually landed again with the post office, but it wasn't before three or four months had rolled by living hand-to-mouth, working as a casual for a freight company, then a laborer for the local Bekins agent, then a warehouseman for Northern Star Mills. His off-hours found him pedaling a battered Columbia three-speed round and about through town in search of a place—the perfect place—to raise up two boys.

～～～

Crossing a bridge on Highway 32 one day, he turned left at the old Hacienda Restaurant with its whitewashed stucco arches and savory aromas wafting from dishes he knew he couldn't enjoy on the pittance he had in his pocket. He headed west down a worn and windy strip of pavement that tunneled through oaks and sycamores and past sublime cottages with lovely lawns and gardens. He'd gone about half a mile when he came across a for sale sign fixed to a white three-rail fence.

For the next week and a half, he pedaled out that avenue every day after work.

"Honeybee," he finally wrote in a letter. "I think I've stumbled onto something. Walking distance from town." He described five-and-a-half acres of almonds and fruit trees with a long driveway to a shaded farmhouse with some workable outbuildings. The parcel fronted on a whispering creek. "It may not be Paradise," he concluded, "but it's close."

Mom wrote back: "I'll pack the car."

Charlie and Rex 1957

RAIN-SOAKED LITTLE BOY.
Ranchcraft blue jeans. From J C Penney. Old downtown store. Muddy cuffs and knees. And black canvas shoes. Maybe Keds? And a white t-shirt caked with mud. Stuck to me.
Dripping wet.
Excited.
Standing in the kitchen. Linoleum floor. Little red brick tile pattern. Muddy footprints leading to a puddle around me.
"We was throwin' sticks . . ."
"We were . . ." Grammar correction. The life-long job of every mother.
"But . . ." Out of breath. "Rex . . . Charlie's dog? . . . He 'ould chase 'em! An' bring 'em back!"
"Out in that rain?"
"Yeah, and . . ." Tears homogenized on my rain-spattered face.
"Charlie, he threw one inta the creek!"
"The creek?"

"Charlie, he got scared... afraid for Rex."

"Yeah, an' Rex, he chased it! Right inta the water!"
Rubbing both eyes with muddy knuckles.
"That water's really moving!"
Breath. "An' Rex he went in an' tried to get the stick!"
Finger wiped under nose.
"Charlie, he got scared..." Another breath. "... afraid for Rex." A swallow. A gulp. "He hollered sumthun and chased after him."

I pointed with my thumb over my shoulder.
"Rex, he's on the patio."

I don't think I remember Mother asking a bunch more about Charlie before she flew out the door.

If she did, I don't remember what I answered.

I do know that all at once, I found myself alone in the kitchen, standing in a puddle.

Shivering.

~~~~

Mr. and Mrs. Deaver lived around the corner from us with Charlie and his little sister and their dog, Rex. The firemen found Charlie lodged under a tree fallen across the swollen creek just past the Rose Avenue bridge. For quite a while, Mom made Dad drive us quietly past the Deaver house. Several times. "Showing respect," she said.

Rose Avenue Bridge (Courtesy T. Allread)

Pretty soon, the Deavers moved away, and Mom wouldn't let me go near the creek for a long time.

Oranges, Peppermint Sticks and Coca-Cola *1959*

CHICO'S KNIGHTS OF COLUMBUS HALL STOOD AS A testament to days gone by. Early in the century, the manor was raised up on donated ground walking distance from town. Once pristine white with black trim, it stood as a beacon amidst acres of wheat and almonds. By the late 1950s, however, while not falling into disrepair, but not fully maintained, the building was little more than an aging gymnasium—a princess never to become queen—a place groups rented when they couldn't afford the elegant Acorn Room at the Oaks Hotel downtown.

The inside was vast and poorly lit and smelled like old, cold dust. Framed pictures of important people hung on the walls here and there. An American flag on a pole was propped into one corner next to an upright piano. Bare planking served as a floor, the finish worn through from countless dance events, potlucks, receptions, wakes and community get-togethers.

Several doors led from this cavernous space to coat closets and anterooms. Each door bore yellowed paint where any paint was left; each was equipped with a tarnished metal doorknob. And those doorknobs were always locked no matter how many times a curious little hand twisted and pulled to gain entry or simply peek inside. Spying through the skeleton keyholes, I thought everything in those chambers behind the doors was dark, mysterious, forbidden and, therefore, wonderful.

Positioned between two of those doors on the largest of the interior walls was a great curtained stage with stairs leading up one side and down the other.

~~~~

Once a year, on the Saturday just before Christmas, the place would teem with postal families—families of the guys who carried the holiday mail—gathering for cheer, heaping plates of sweet, saucy spaghetti topped with a buttery slab of French bread, and a visit with Santa.

While somebody's mom played Christmas songs on the upright, the kids my age and those both a little older and much younger skated around the great hall, up and down the aisles between the rows of oil-clothed tables, sliding in stockinged feet. Soon one of us would pick up a painful sliver from the planking. There'd be a shriek. The injured party would repair to his or her particular mother who would remove the wood piece with surgical precision using only pointy fingernails. The object lesson of our frolic's consequences lasted about five minutes, and soon we'd again glide across the bare wood floor.

While others observed the surgery or tugged at the doors and peeked through those keyholes, I would find Don VanMeter, the man who carried our mail, look up at him, and say, "Hello." With a bottle of Miller High Life in one hand, he'd rub my burr-cut head with the other and say, "Hello yourself." Then I'd go find Glenn Walker, the neighbor whom everyone called "Johnny" and get similar treatment. Bill George and Dandy Rogers responded in the same way as did the countless others who took this evening to eat and celebrate before returning to their holiday-heavy duties, ensuring that Christmas would arrive on time in Chico.

Dad's closest workmate, an unmarried man named Terrence that Mom thought was a "real catch," wasn't on hand. I searched for him, but I couldn't find him.

~~~~~

When the bell rang for dinner, we sat down, family style, on hard wooden benches pulled close to the long rows of tables. The postmaster stood and offered thanks to the Lord. During grace, most of us kids nibbled at the sweet French bread until our respective mothers slapped our hands, glaring down at us as only mothers can. Next, we'd dig into that saucy spaghetti, having been admonished by the man who'd so recently been in conversation with the Lord: "San-tee Claus won't come 'til you've cleaned up your plate."

An eternity passed while we ate the meal. Then, dramatically, the lights went out. An audible whoosh emptied the air from the room as everyone's surprised breath sucked in. All was silent save for an infant or two. A tiny crease of light showed from beneath the velveteen curtains, and after a time appropriate for manufacturing a little more drama, the curtains split.

There sat Santa.

We cheered.

Santa read "The Night Before Christmas." Then all of us kids lined up—littlest ones first—climbed onto the stage and received our presents from Santa and his helper: a peppermint stick, a naval orange, and a six-and-a-half-ounce bottle of Coca-Cola. Santa's helper, always one of Terrence's girlfriends, hurried us off the stage so the procession would keep moving.

Once back on the floor, the oldest of the boys placed penny bets about something embossed on the bottom of their soda bottles. I turned mine over but was far more interested with what was inside. Some of the girls broke the ends off their peppermint sticks and poked them through the rind of their navel oranges, using the candy as a straw to draw out the juice. The kids my age and younger just wandered about, trying to negotiate holding three precious gifts while walking across the slick wood floor in stockinged feet and grinning because we'd all just seen "San-tee Claus."

Christmas was here.

~~~

One holiday, a few years later, I recall Dad coming home from his Saturday rounds and telling Mom, "I'm not feeling so hot. Why don't you just run on over to the Knights of Columbus and go ahead and enjoy yourself." He gestured with the

> **"I looked to my left where Mom was sitting, but she was gone."**

hand holding a half-full bottle of Miller High Life. "Take the kids and go and have yourself a good time."

Dad wasn't coming!

The hall was as big as ever, as dusty as ever, but somehow colder than usual this time. I sat on a bench next to Mom, choosing not to skate on the wooden floor. I didn't nibble at the French bread atop my mound of spaghetti while thanks was offered. I only wished that the postmaster would ask God to somehow send Dad to the party. How could Dad miss this? What if he was dying? He must be! How could he miss this? I stabbed and twisted my dinner and let it grow cold.

Then the lights went out. When the curtain opened, as the kids lined up, I looked to my left where Mom was sitting, but she was gone.

Gone!

Now, too big to cry or yell out—the year prior, I'd won six or eight cents from the other boys because my Coke bottle had the word "Louisville" embossed on its bottom—I sat on the wooden bench like a stone. As the kids readied to walk across the stage, it seemed that the room had grown even colder. My eyes filmed over, and I blinked to clear them. I'm not sure why. It'd just be a haggard procession of silly little children getting a peppermint stick, an orange and a bottle of Coke from a costumed Terrence—I figured that out last year—and his current girlfriend would hurry them off the stage to keep the line moving.

Sitting among the long rows of tables, I was the only kid left on the floor. I swiped a finger across my eyes and watched. On the stage, Santa slipped a white-gloved paw across his helper's rump as she passed. His helper glanced back at him and smiled coyly. I shook my head and rubbed my eyes again, this time real hard.

It was Mom! Mom was up there! Mom was San-tee Claus's helper!

Like peering through a keyhole into a fully lit room, I understood a number of other things—frightening things, things steeped in an angry, new reality. I wanted to bolt from the room, through the hall's old front door, out through the orchards into the winter night and never come back. Something was pounding inside my chest as if I had. I dropped my head into my folded arms on the sticky oilcloth. In this self-imposed darkness, I muffled the raucous laughter and cheers of the postal families and hoped to God that no one could hear me cry.

After the procession, Mom brought me an orange, a candy cane and a Coke, which I pushed to one side. Later, while one little kid pounded on the piano and the others resumed skating, I helped clean the hall with Don and Johnny and the other adults.

With the task complete, we got into the car and headed home. Driving through the winter blackness, I couldn't form the words that would ask what was going on between my mother and my dad's best buddy.

We arrived home to a cold house with a dark Christmas tree standing in the corner of the living room. I headed to my room, swinging the door closed, not caring how loud it slammed. Fully clothed, I collapsed atop my bed. My throat tightened. My eyes burned in the darkness. Every sound from outside my window, every nighttime itch and tickle held sleep at bay. My mind raced back to that moment of Mom and "San-tee" on the stage and kept rerunning it like a frightening scene from *Fantasia* or the *Wizard of Oz*. Wide awake in the gloom, I thought about climbing out of bed, sneaking into the living room and tearing that damned tree down.

~~~~

That next morning, I awoke to the smell of bacon frying in the kitchen. A rumpled Santa suit lay draped over the couch across from the tree. Bleary eyed, I picked up the bulky red coat, cuddled it a bit and dragged it behind me as I wandered into the kitchen.

"How'd you think your father did playing Santa last night?" Mom asked, cracking an egg into a pool of bacon grease in cast-iron pan.

By this time, Dad was off to the post office to make rare Sunday rounds, ensuring Christmas would arrive in Chico on time.

The Great Horseapple Wars of the Late 1950s *1959*

TOWNCRAFT T-SHIRTS FOR LITTLE BOYS WERE THREE for 99 cents at J C Penney. Ranchcraft blue jeans were under six bucks. These two items comprised the apparel *du jour* for all the neighborhood boys engaged in the Saturday afternoon Horseapple Wars of about 1958 or 59.

Next door to where I grew up, our neighbors, the Calverts, had about an acre and a half. Their property had been carved out of a seven-acre almond orchard, and we'd moved into the larger chunk. In point of fact, their house had been the parcel's farmhouse, and what became our place used to be the barn. Behind their house, a weathered and worn pecky-cedar fence corralled a dozen or so aging almond trees and a retired circus pony named Tiny. Mr. Calvert actually used to own a little one-ring circus, and their property was strewn with an amazing and magical collection of circus performance goods and props: sections of the wooden ring, a three-and-a-half-foot tall wooden ball, various bolts and folds of once-gaily decorated tent canvas, cages previously inhabited by

The Great Horseapple Wars of the Late 1950s   15

Tiny and the twins (Courtesy T. Allread)

monkeys—all stored in a derelict 40-foot trailer with faded paint reading "A. Calvert & Sons Shows." And then there was Tiny.

Tiny was a curious attraction for all of us neighborhood boys. He never was allowed to venture outside the confines of the cedar plank fence. Tall for a pony, he was palomino in color and skittish as all hell. No one could ride him. Inside the fenced area, our little gang watched—more than once—as one of the Calvert twins charged up to Tiny, grabbed his mane and flipped himself onto the pony's back to be summarily dumped on the other side of the beast with nary a nicker. The kid, Calvie—we called both boys Calvie because they were identical twins and neither I nor anyone else could tell them apart—always popped to his feet appearing unscathed, but we knew it hurt every time we witnessed it, and I knew I was never going to try to ride Tiny. I'm sure Nilley and Musty and anybody else who was present thought the same thing.

"What good is a horse you can't ride?" I asked out loud with a laugh. Then something hit me just behind and below my left ear. And the wars were on.

~~~~~

Horse manure can be used for many things. In Rancho Days, the early *Californios* would mix clay, manure and water and place the concoction into rectangular molds to dry, forming adobe bricks. The partially digested hay or straw in the horse droppings helped bind the mud bricks together, adding strength to the brick and stability to the missions and ranch houses of our state's earliest European settlements. In more recent times, manure has been bagged and sold at garden shops and home improvement outlets as an inexpensive mulching material: two drawbacks being the smell and the occasional sprouting of a healthy crop of alfalfa or wheat straw among the family's pumpkins, watermelons, row crops or dichondra.

> "Horse manure can be used for many things."

The Great Horseapple Wars of the Late 1950s

But back in the late '50s and in our little neighborhood, a favored use of Tiny's prodigious product was as a projectile. A missile. An orb perfect for chucking at the nearest kid's noggin. A little smaller than an official size and weight Little League hard ball, a horseapple possessed a density light enough that no one struck was ever really hurt.

~~~~

I slapped the portion of my neck where I'd been hit. A bit of sweetly pungent goo and a few alfalfa fibers stuck to my fingertips. One of the Calvies slipped across my range of vision. At my feet rested an amalgamation of horseapples piled curiously like a picture of cannon balls I'd seen in my old Davy Crockett book. Remembering the Alamo, I grabbed a fat one from the top of the pile and flung wildly. It splattered on the black trunk of an almond tree. I reached for a reload as one whizzed over my head. Rising, I was hit square between the shoulders of my white Towncraft T-shirt. I spun, threw and missed again. Another one hit me on the shoulder accompanied by a shrill laugh. Reaching for another, I rose to be clocked once, twice, three more times: volleys were incoming from every direction, as were the gales of laughter.

I'm certain that I grazed one or two of the neighborhood boys—maybe Musty, maybe Nilley, maybe one of the Calvies. But the battle was soon lost to wriggling children, each falling to the orchard floor, succumbing to the involuntary responses uncontrollable guffaws portend.

About the time the mirth died down, another round landed near somebody. A second skirmish ensued. Then a third. Then a fourth.

Finally, in the dying afternoon light, someone's mother called, using that classic musical minor third indicating dinner was ready, and it was time to head home.

Horseapple residue does not readily wash out of white cotton Towncraft T-shirts nor Ranchcraft blue jeans, according to Mom. She more than admonished us that Tiny's droppings were best left on the ground, adding, "I'll be damned if I'm going to have you ruin a perfectly good 33-cent shirt every Saturday afternoon."

But we didn't listen. Our neighborhood consisted of over a half dozen boys, more than one of whom was willing to engage in battle as long as Tiny was willing to produce munitions, regardless of what his or any other kid's mother had to say about things. Each initial, singular volley led to a donnybrook of flying dung and laughter even though the consequences ramped up with every new occurrence.

The finality of the wars came about like this, quoting my frustrated mother: "One day all you'll have is those . . . those . . . befouled, stinking T-shirts to wear to school, and then what will the others think?"

"That we had some fun playing war with Tiny's . . ." I chose not to say the word.

Over the giggles of the others, there was heard an audible gasp. Mom wheeled from us, plucked the phone receiver from the kitchen wall and dialed. The conversation was short. She hung up and dialed again. Then again. Like a latter-day Paul Revere but without a steed, Mom had seen to it that all the mothers in the neighborhood were of common mind and purpose. Turning back to us, we were sternly warned—something akin to the end of life as we then knew it—and sent on our way. The great Horseapple Wars had come to an end. We would need to find something else, something less filthy, to do.

~~~

So we did.

Musty lived four or five doors down. His house was newer and trimmer and cleaner, and a bit better kept than ours or that of Calverts. Newest in the neighborhood, Musty's house had been hand built by his own father. It stood as a monument to pride and craftsmanship and attention to detail from the brick chimney that towered over the shake roof to the pristine clover lawn bordered in a hedge of blueberry bushes—blueberry bushes whose fruit came to ripeness—and over-ripeness—about mid-October.

An over-ripe blueberry is much smaller than a regulation horseapple. Its smooth flesh is much more difficult to grip. It doesn't sail as far when flicked or thrown.

Musty's smaller, suburban-sized front yard would prove to be a fine venue for what was to come.

Playin' Hooky from God 1959

SUNDAY BREAKFAST WAS SUPPOSED TO BE SPECIAL. NOT the weekday Shredded Wheat or Cheerios bathed in sugary milk, but sausage and eggs or pancakes or waffles drowned in Log Cabin syrup. But brother Beebo and I never got to savor Sunday breakfast. Instead, we were told to eat up or we'd be late. When finished, we were commanded to brush our teeth, put on our good corduroys and best Little Yankee shoes and pile into the backseat of the car. Mom would pilot us the mile or so downtown, double park in front of the First Baptist Church, give each of our cheeks a pinch, say, "Now you boys be good," then wheel the car round the corner and out of sight. Sometimes it seemed like she was in a hurry to get rid of us.

The First Baptist Church of Chico had stood between Broadway and Salem on Fifth Street forever as far as Beebo and I knew. It was a big, weathered building sided with vertical wooden boards painted a chalky brown that would rub off on your good clothes if you leaned against it. Colored glass

Old First Baptist Church (Courtesy First Baptist Church of Chico)

windows were framed in pointy, religious arches, although on several, one or more of the pieces of glass were cracked or missing. The edges of brick stairs leading to the front doors were worn to nearly round over years and years of use. Inside, just past the entry, a huge room like an auditorium had a big sloping floor filled with row upon row of wooden benches that drained toward a raised stage with a higher place from which to look down on people. It was where all the big people met. But it was a place Beebo and I couldn't enter because neither Mom nor Dad ever attended. Every Sunday, we'd stand in the double doorway to the big room and peer into its dark depths until we were bumped out of the way and channeled upstairs with all the other kids. Upstairs was where we went to Sunday School.

At the top of the stairs was an endless hallway with doors opening to rooms set up for preschoolers, kindergartners and grade levels paired off by twos. With my hair butchwaxed in place, I entered the first-second–grade room and Beebo went to third-fourth. At seven—nearly eight—years of age, I was older than most of the kids in the room, and, because the First Baptist Church served all of town, not just where I went to school, I knew only one other kid in our group, a nasty little girl named Rebecca. She was in my class at real school. She'd always cross her eyes and stick her tongue out at me *all the time*. I didn't like her.

The classroom floor was worn-out wood partly covered by a threadbare piece of carpet with frayed, fuzzy edges. A huge, black piano was shoved against one wall. Three unmatched tables were surrounded by a collection of hand-me-down little kids' chairs. The tops of the tables felt like grit and were covered in something like linoleum and dotted with dried globs of white glue. It seemed that every time I found myself coloring in a shepherd or a tree or one of Jesus's robes, my crayon would hang up on a glue glob beneath my paper and make a skip or a spot darker than I wanted. Or maybe the crayon point would break. Dad, when something like that happened, said "Dammit" a lot. I found this was not the place to sound like Dad and tried not to wince when the ruler rapped across my knuckles.

> **“Lovely though this may have sounded to others, it seemed pretty much like where Beebo and I lived every day.”**

I don't recall whether the teacher was a young person or an old one, although remembering the rap on my knuckles, she was probably old. After playing "Jesus Loves Me" on the untuned old upright, she turned on the piano stool and gathered us at her feet for a story. One I particularly remember spoke of a place called Eden where the land was verdant green, and a lovely stream of pure, "living" water trickled past. There were flowers in the dale and fruit free for the picking. Birds and beasts and frogs and butterflies and all the animals of the world grazed in peace.

Lovely though this may have sounded to others in the class, it seemed pretty much like where Beebo and I lived every day. Our five acres faced a creek. In the front and side yards, we grew peaches and plums and even apples like the one in the story. As far as birds of the air and beasts of the field went, quail and pheasants made our almond orchard out back their home, and next door, Mr. Calvert once trapped a raccoon. Eden indeed.

Beebo and I both quickly grew tired of the sing-songy little kids' rhymey hymns and Bible stories about lambs along with pages of outlined lambs we were supposed to color in but without any white crayons available. The circumstance felt way too much like sitting in a classroom when we'd already sat in real classrooms with real teachers for five days the previous week. The only thing missing was a spelling test.

~~~~~

Our charge was to attend, behave, and then walk home. On one of those walks, Beebo and I compared notes.

"Wha'd'ja you learn?"

"Nothin'. How 'bout you?"

"Nothin'. Got my knuckles rapped again . . ."

"Wha'd'ja do, dummy?"

"Nothin'!"

So the next Sunday, we didn't go to Sunday School. Instead, we headed up the stairs but slipped past our classrooms. At the far end of the hall was another door. We cracked it open and peeked in. Another stairway! We glanced over our shoulders. There was no one behind us. First and second graders—my group—were already singing "Jesus Loves Me."

We tiptoed up the stairs. On this third floor, another passageway stretched the length of and then round the back of the sanctuary. Trying all the ancient glass knobs, we found that one of the doors opened into a room packed tight with organ pipes. Once inside, we peeked through the pipes and peered down, scanning the crowd, seeing who we might recognize. Beebo spotted his regular teacher, Miss Smithers, pointed at her and stifled a giggle. I saw that Harvey, the grocer, was there, and so was Hap Andrews, the insurance man who lived in our neighborhood. We settled in, spying for people we knew, knowing they couldn't see us wormed in between all those pipes. From our vantage point on high, we saw everyone and witnessed everything they were doing down there: fidgets, muffled coughs, whispers, sideways glances, even some secret hand holding. *Miss Smithers!*

Somewhere, a muffled speech—sometimes soft, sometimes roaring—came from someone we could not see. He must have been directly below us.

Pretty soon, everybody rose. Suddenly, the pipes of the organ blasted. The hiss and roar rattled our bones and set our innards to churning. I'm sure our screams were involuntary, but I doubt anyone down below could hear them—or the slamming of the chamber door—due to the crescendo of the music. As the thundering song was joined by voices, we rumbled further down the hall, but not so quickly that we couldn't investigate what might be hidden behind some more of the creaky doors. One room held tablecloths or robes. One had stacks of books all the same. One, a tangle of old chairs. But most were either empty or cluttered with stuff probably long forgotten. They all smelled of stale moisture and darkness and dust.

By the time the hymn had subsided, we'd circled around toward the street side of the building, where another door led to a little square room with another set of steps. A set of thick ropes reached from a hole in the floor up into the shadowy darkness above. The steps angled upward to a landing. From the landing the steps became rungs somehow cemented into the brick wall, rungs that led to a trap door in the ceiling. The view from the top, we figured, must be terrific.

Beebo was older, but I rassled him aside and went first. Using the top of my head, I pushed through the hatch, cracking it enough that a little sunlight washed in. At that moment, the ropes began to move up and down, and within seconds bells rang out that must have been heard to the furthest corners of our little city. It was deafening. I think I screamed another scream, but I couldn't hear myself and groped for my ears. I tumbled backward down the ladder-like stairs to the highest of the landings. Beebo grabbed my shoulders and pulled me up. We stood there, trembling, ears covered with palms, eventually looking through one of those pointy arched things, this one with slats angled down. Way below, we could see people leaving the old building. Everyone was gathering out front, shaking hands and greeting one another. I saw Rebecca. Her mom was giving Becca a hug. I wished I had a wad of gum to flick down on her. She'd never know where it came from.

As the bells stopped peeling, all the people just drifted off like mustard seeds on a soft breeze.

Church was over.

Beebo and I looked at each other, each thinking the same thoughts.

"What if they lock the place up and we get stuck inside?" I said.

"What if someone catches us up here?" Beebo said.

"What if God catches us up here?" I said.

"God already knows where we are. He always does."

The thought chilled me. Probably Beebo, too.

We slithered down the stairs and through the darkened hall like the serpents we knew we were. Finding a ground floor door that opened to the outside, we slipped out to a back parking area and hid behind a nearby camellia bush until it seemed folks had left. In a very few moments, a tall, distinguished-looking man in a gray suit exited that same door. There was a white square on his funny looking collar where a tie would normally be. A silky black robe was bunched and draped over his arm. Standing on the stoop, he reached into his shirt pocket a retrieved a pack of cigarettes. Taking, apparently, the last one out, he wadded up the empty pack and tossed it on the ground. Lighting up, he saw us behind the camellia and said, "Well, hello, boys." Then he opened the driver's side of a Lincoln Continental, gave us a wink, and drove away.

In hushed tones, I asked, "Do you suppose that was God?"

"I dunno," Beebo said, shaking his head. "But he did seem to know we were here."

~~~~

In wide-eyed silence, we walked the 35-minute route through town and along the creek to home.

Mom was waiting for us at the foot of the driveway.

I'd learned the word damnation in Sunday School. I recall it having something to do with what happened to people who didn't go to Sunday School. But I'd never been exposed to the word consternation. However, with Mom's facial expression chiseled into my memory from that Sunday, I'll always grasp the precise meaning of the term.

Mom shifted a narrow, icy gaze back and forth between each of her sons. The cold moment of silence seemed like it lasted an hour. Then, using a low, near-whisper, that particular tone only my mother could muster, she informed us that we couldn't attend the First Baptist Church Sunday School anymore.

Damnation was surely next.

One New Year's Eve *1960*

I STOOD BARE FOOTED ON THE CURVED RED CONCRETE walk that led to a front door we used only on occasion. It couldn't have been more than 32 degrees outside that night. The sky was clear and every star in the galaxy was out, celebrating the first time I would see midnight come and go. My flannel pj's and white terry cloth robe did little to insulate me from the winter cold, and I should have gone back inside to find my slippers. But the hour was near, and I would not miss this stroke of midnight.

At some point, Beebo or some kid from down the road showed up with a flashlight, shining it across the yard, up into the branches of the sycamore trees at the end of the house or into everybody's faces. I wanted it turned off. I wanted to see what the night was like. Especially this night. Finally, after enough of my caterwauling, Mom or Dad saw that the flashlight's dancing beam was stilled, and, again, all that could be seen heavenward were those stars framed in the foreground by the now wicked-looking bare winter branches of the sycamore trees at either end of the house.

Gazing at the heavens, I wondered what or who might be looking back. I figured maybe God was up there somewhere since that's what I'd been led to believe in Sunday School. I never considered that God might have his hands full with other earthly or celestial matters. I simply imagined if I found just the right star, I might see him peeking back at me from behind it. Maybe even winking. So I stood in front of the house on the frigid sidewalk thinking about God and other things. The cement's cold coursed upward through my feet and legs causing shivers and shakes. I lifted one foot, and then the other, tightened the terry cloth robe under my chin, and peered upward until my neck hurt.

I wondered about the distance to those stars. I wondered about the passage of time and how long there'd actually been time. I wondered about what might change when midnight marked the beginning of a new day, a new year, and, although I didn't know what a decade was, a new one of those. I held my breath and waited for this midnight's stroke.

Then, off in the distance, back toward town where streetlights more than likely muted the glittery nature of the stars, popping could be heard. Fireworks, low on the horizon, were joined by faint huzzahs and yelps. Clyde, the fox terrier from next door, began to bark, and soon his dog buddies from throughout the neighborhood chorused in.

But beyond the report of Clyde or his colleagues, nothing in particular seemed to have changed. The stars still twinkled

"I wondered about the passage of time..."

just like in the nursery jingle. It was still really cold out. The world was still dark. But I was pretty sure the sun would rise in the morning like it always had. The passage through midnight apparently meant nothing. Likewise, the passing of one year into the next.

Presently, I found myself under a heap of covers. Mom or Dad had embraced my shoulders, and after saying, "Well, there it is," pointed me back through the front door we only used on occasion and toddled me off to bed. Wrapped tightly in those blankets, I rubbed my frozen feet against one another and up and down my flannel-covered ankles hoping they would warm up enough that I could fall asleep.

~~~~

As midnight passed, the 1950s drew to a close. And as I watched, the '60s, with all its mystery and possibility, slipped in under a starlit, dark cover. There I stood, an eight-year-old in flannel jammies and numb feet, wondering how what lay ahead might be different from what had already happened, yet as certain as an eight-year-old could be, at least from all I'd gained that night, that everything would remain just about the same.

At the Livestock Auction *1960*

IN A SMALL TOWN JUST ACROSS THE RIVER, THERE WAS an auction yard, a place to buy cattle and horses and all kinds of livestock.

"Up this way," Dad said. "We're gonna be country. We need go see what that's all about."

A year or two removed from the LA Basin, Dad was gonna be country. Mom, I'll always suspect, was just along for the ride because she said, "We're not going to buy a damned cow."

~~~~

Dad wheeled our Ford Ranchwagon onto an acres-large gravel parking lot, disappearing amongst cattle trucks and stock trailers. A maze of pens and chutes ran next to the parking area and hooked into the backside of a battered old building about the size of the gymnasium at Beebo's junior high. The whole place smelled of manure and hay and dust.

Breaking away from Mom and Dad, I climbed on a fence rail. I was looking for a donkey and wondered if one might be in a pen ready for sale. Tiny, the neighbor's pony, had died a month or so before and his carcass hauled off to the rendering plant south of town. Maybe we could get a donkey, I thought, and use him on backpacking trips and keep him where Tiny had been.

Peering over the top of the weather-beaten rail fence, I could see the humps of cattle backs squeezed tightly together. The animals didn't look at all comfortable. They jostled one another, shifting and groaning, the fence boards bending and creaking in concert with their movement.

A firm grip fell upon my shoulder, and I was pulled down from the fence, summarily receiving a smart slap across the chops. "Don't you run off around this place! You could fall in and get trampled and then what?" It was Mom. "And when we get inside, sit on your hands."

We entered the building with my ear firmly in my mother's grasp. The foyer was dark compared to the parking area outdoors. There were a couple of plywood partitions each masking the entrance to a non-doored restroom. I think there was also a small office, but what caught my attention was the concession area. There were bottles of soda, packages of Wrigley's gum and a selection of candy bars, and it was staffed by a blue-gingham–clad gal who looked a lot like Dorothy Gale, if Aunt Em and Uncle Henry's niece had somehow aged to be a little older than Mom. I couldn't find the words to ask Dad for 15 cents so I could buy a Coca-Cola—no, a Nehi orange since Nehis came in a bigger bottle—and a Payday before I was pulled into the darker confines of the auction arena.

At the Livestock Auction

Along with the shadowy darkness there was a thunderous mix of sounds. Some fast-talking fellow with a big, chrome microphone roared numbers or words my ears were too slow to make out. Added to this was a clunking syncopation of boot heels on wooden bleachers, the murmur of attendees evaluating the stock and the occasional bawl of a sad baby cow.

"Bummer calf," Dad said. "Abandoned by his mother."

I didn't know how Dad might have known this stuff—maybe from watching *Rawhide* on TV—but suddenly I was anxious about being abandoned by Mom. It had happened one Christmas not so very long ago. I rubbed the tender earlobe she'd so recently released.

The route into the arena led through a dim channel between two sets of those bleachers occupied by denim-clad cowboys with those high-heeled boots, which because of the clunky sound they made, I immediately coveted.

"Remember to sit on your hands," my mother repeated above the din.

We had to approach a big enclosure with a dusty dirt floor encircled with metal pipes in order find seats anywhere. This middle part of the room was brightly lit. Inside the corral, some cowboys herded a few head of cattle. We walked around the dusty ring past where the man with the microphone, dressed in a clean plaid shirt and nice straw cowboy hat, was rattling on too rapidly.

"That's the auctioneer," Dad explained, pointing, causing Mom to exclaim: "Don't point!"

" 'Remember to sit on your hands!' I did as commanded. "

Seeing us move by, the auctioneer winked at me as he continued his prattle, so I winked back using both eyes.

Dad nodded toward an open space of seating far up the bleachers. "Over there," he said.

We climbed through spectators clad in weary snap pocketed plaids or faded chambray shirts and equally faded and ranch-worn jeans—and those boots. The further we climbed from the auction ring, the darker things became and the harder it was to see where to put my feet. I hoped I wouldn't step on a cowboy and end up getting drilled by slug from his six-shooter. Soon we reached the spot to settle.

"Remember to sit on your hands!"

I did as commanded.

In time my eyes adjusted, and I began to see the entertainment that was unfolding before me. The livestock—cattle, mostly—was shuttled onto the auction floor through an entry opposite where we'd come in. Wranglers hooted and whistled and rapped the flanks of the beasts with coiled ropes until the gate behind them was closed.

The man with the microphone, the auctioneer, momentarily spoke in a manner I could understand: "Now raise your sights, folks. This here represents a herd of Herefords from the Vina Plain's Somethingerother Ranch out there toward Gerber . . ." I could make out the words but not their meaning.

He rambled on with a sing-songy drawl, making me think that crossing the Sacramento River to get to Orland, California, we'd somehow ended up deep in the heart of Texas. His narrative ended with: "Now what am I bid?" followed by: "Hey gimme fi'dollah, fi'dollah, fi'dollah, ten. Hey, fi'dollah, fi'dollah, fi'dollah. HUP! Now gimme ten dollah, ten dollah, ten dollah, twenty. HUP! Gimme twenty, twenty, twenty..."

It took a while for my ears to catch up with what was going on and a while longer to figure out what "HUP!" meant. But pretty soon, his rapid banter stopped, a sprinkling of applause ran through the crowd and the animals were herded back out through the chute to be replaced by another group. I finally got the drift of the auctioneer's chatter and began to link the "HUP!" with some movement in the crowd caught by one of three or four cowboys in better blue jeans, with plaid shirts and crisp straw hats matching those of the auctioneer.

Mom wasn't sitting on her hands, nor was Dad, but both of my hands were planted underneath my butt as a third, a fourth and a fifth group of animals came in and departed. It didn't seem fair. Then the inevitable occurred: A piece of lint or dust or maybe a horsefly settled inside my nose. I reached up to excavate it.

"Sit on your hands!" Mom said, her voice trembling in panic while the auctioneer rattled, "Fitty, fitty, fitty, fitty."

I quickly slipped my hand under the seat of my pants, but it was too late. "HUP!" The auctioneer was pointing right at me. Somehow, he must have known we'd arrived in a Ranchwagon. "Sold!" he bellowed into the big, chrome microphone. My stomach felt like a rock had dropped into it. I'd just bought a herd of Holsteins. I looked at Mom, mortified. The smattering of applause rippled through the arena and I was about to cry when a skinny, older gentleman seated behind us stood up and took a bow.

Dad laughed and put his arm around me. I felt Mom's glare boring through both of us.

~~~~~

I returned my hands to under my butt while I figured out the system. Sellers brought livestock: cattle, horses, pigs, sheep—sheep entering the ring were met with a collective groan—then the auctioneer gave a little description and burst into his call. Spotters pointed out buyers, and over the course of a few minutes, a deal was done. My hands grew numb as I sat on them for about three hours watching all of this take place. As it turns out, there would be no donkeys offered this day. Mom probably wouldn't have let us get one anyway.

When it came time to leave, Dad asked if I wanted a Coca-Cola or a Nehi. I picked the Nehi because it was bigger. Dad gave the Dorothy Gale look-alike a dime and placed the wet, slippery bottle in my still tingly, numbed, asleep hand, from which it fell to the floor, rolling under the counter and leaving an orange trail in its path. For the second time, I almost cried, but Dorothy offered up another, saying, "On the house, buckaroo."

~~~~~

Before long, we were in the old Ford heading home.

And for the next couple of weeks, Dad gently—until she'd had enough—chided Mom for thinking a seasoned auctioneer would be dumb enough to sell a herd of dairy cattle to an eight-year-old kid who happened to be picking his nose up near the back row of the auction house. Meanwhile, I scoured the poultry and livestock sections of our local paper's classified ads looking for a donkey to pen up in the neighbor's back forty and carry my stuff on hikes.

But a donkey never came up in the classifieds, and pretty soon I got interested in go-carts.

The Rope Swing 1960

ONE SUMMER AFTERNOON WE BUILT A ROPE SWING with an old Firestone tire we'd dug out of the creek bank. We had to toss a line over a branch about a mile up in the sycamore tree on the west side of the house. Didn't get it over at first. Had to tie something on the end of the rope so we could get the heft to fling it over.

First, we tried a smooth, old river rock with a big, fresh chip in one side that had just been plowed up out back in the orchard. Every couple of tosses the rock slipped out of the loop we'd cinched around it. Once it hit Danny Vanella—Nilley we called him—on the side of the head, and he went home crying.

We switched to Dad's hammer, which I'd snuck from his workshop, a beautiful, old, leather-handled Estwing with its grip worn to a shine from years of various around-the-house jobs. Dad came pedaling home—he rode his bike to work: we only had one car—and told us that wasn't what the hammer was for. We rightly figured he meant crow bars, vice grips, pipe wrenches, hand axes—just about anything else that could be found in the shop—as well.

There was a galvanized metal bucket out back of the house that Mom used exclusively for hauling ash from the Franklin stove out to the orchard. I swiped it from where Mom kept it. We tied one end of the rope around its bail.

Muster, another kid from the neighborhood, said we should fill it "this much" full with water. So we did. Old Musty swung the bucket like the pendulum on the cuckoo clock in our dining room, back and forth, back and forth. Each time a little bit further. Soon he was making great, sweeping circles with the water bucket at the end of the rope.

Then, using this magical boy judgment that some kids possess, he let the rope slip and race through his dirty palm at just the right instant. The bucket rocketed skyward, arcing and clearing the branch on the very first throw and falling to earth with the water exploding out of its busted bottom when the bucket hit the ground.

Soaked hurrahs were sounded all around. And slaps on the back. Musty was a genius! A real whiz!

Nilley, by now, had come back—a red bandanna wrapped around his forehead—and stood a distance away at the property line leaning on the white rail fence.

Both ends of the rope were in kid hands. While I tied the muddy, black-sidewalled Firestone to one end of the rope, Calvie, one of the twins from next door, shinnied up the great sycamore tree and wiggled out on to the limb. He hoisted up the other end of the rope, did a couple of wraps with it

The rope swing

and tugged on it a couple of times. Finding things secure enough to suit the mind of an experienced boy of 10 or 11, Calvie dangled his legs off the limb, found the rope with first one foot, then the other, slipped his butt off the branch and descended the rope hand over hand.

The once derelict tire now hung about two and a half feet off the ground, and since Nilley looked so forlorn but so interested, Calvie waved him over. In the gathering dusk, he enjoyed the first ride.

I don't think we used that rope swing for more than the waning hours of that summer day and a little bit of the next. To be sure, we spent more time engineering the swing than we ever did riding it.

We get together now, the fellows of that industry—except for Nilley. AIDS overtook him when he was just 26 or so. The rest of us, Calvie and Musty and me, we used to get together and drink beer and smoke cheap cigars. Proving we're big boys now.

We talk about good jobs and bad politics, failed marriages and lingering loves. And tell a few jokes. Never have talked about the rope swing in the sycamore tree. Hell, I may be the only one who even remembers the whole event.

I kept meaning to ask Calvie, when I saw him, this question: if he could shinny up a tree to secure a dangling line to a branch about a mile up in the air, why'd we dedicate an otherwise perfectly fine summer's afternoon to trying to toss that damned rope over the tree limb in the first place?

But by the time I remembered the question, the party had broken up and everybody'd gone home.

My First Two-Wheeler   1960

"NOW YOU OWN A SCHWINN BICYCLE!" THE ANNOUNCE-ment began. Coiled into a tiny tube and tied tightly with curling ribbon, the owner's manuals for our new Schwinn three-speeds hung among the branches of the Christmas tree like ornaments.

December 25th dawned, and brother Beebo and I awoke early and raced to the tree. For Beebo, 11, and me, not yet nine, the magic of Christmas morning was more than imagined. It was real. We tittered and giggled and fingered the bounty of wrapped packages until Mom and Dad wandered in, bleary-eyed. Their arrival signaled something akin to the bugler's call at Churchill Downs. Within minutes I was in possession of a new cap six-shooter, a felt cowboy hat, a copy of *Hans Brinker or the Silver Skates* and, I suppose, a Mom-sewn shirt or some hand-knit mittens. Likewise for Beebo. It wasn't until the last of the wrapping paper had floated to rest on the floor that Mom and Dad reached into the branches and pulled out the coiled manuals from the tree. Cluelessly, we leafed through them briefly and shrugged, thinking, "That's really odd. We don't own Schwinn bicycles." We tossed the brochures amongst the mountain of wrapping paper and returned to pointing our six-shooters at each other.

Breakfast was served on the former screened-in porch between the kitchen and the patio, and it wasn't until halfway through a waffle laced with bacon and drowned in syrup that Mom's patience ran out. "Why don't you boys just stop and look?" she asked with a familiar tone of exasperation in her voice.

She was pointing to the patio. Outside the window rested two brand-new Schwinn bicycles: The Racer models with Sturmey-Archer three-speed gears and skinny tires beneath pinched front metal fenders. These bikes were the likes of which big kids—*college kids!*— and adults rode. *Heck!* Dad commuted to work at the post office *every day* on a Schwinn Traveler model quite similar to these beauties.

Still clad in pajamas, we bolted out the back door. Beebo claimed a big blue one and a slightly smaller red one waited for me. We kicked up the kickstands, pointed them to the gravel drive and began pedaling out toward the road. Pride of the neighborhood, we now had means of personal transportation to and from school, over to the CARD Pool, down to town for a Saturday matinee at the El Rey, on rides through Bidwell Park with Mom and Dad and the freedom to go just about anywhere in the world we wanted.

"Why don't you boys just stop and look?"

Later that summer, we used Dad's old Ford tractor and a wooden skid to grade a racetrack around the perimeter of the four and a half acres of almonds out back of the house. It seemed like a good idea at the time, but the narrow tires of our Racers didn't handle the dust and dirt clods of the orchard too well. One day, a neighbor kid named Lewis Tubbs came by on his new Sting-Ray. A Sting-Ray was a bicycle built on a tiny frame using small wheels with fat tires. It sported an elongated "banana seat" molded to look like tuck 'n' roll upholstery. Its high-rise handlebars wore sparkly grips the same color as the frame. No three-speed, this single-geared, coaster-brake marvel took to the dust and mud like it was engineered for it. On our racecourse, Lewis stood on the pedals and cranked them round and round. When he came to the curve at the far corner of the orchard, he boldly put his foot down and turned like he was pivoting on a peg. Then down the straightaway he'd race. Neither Beebo nor I could catch him.

Awe struck; we knew what we needed to do. Much as we were to revere our big Schwinn Racers, all of a sudden, they simply didn't cut the mustard.

~~~~

Vern Pullin had owned a bicycle dealership in downtown Chico for about 160 years. It was said that the local Mechoopda Indians bought bikes from him before the white people settled the area. Why would we *not* believe this? His shop was located at Eighth and Broadway. The front room was a neatly arranged row of Schwinn's latest offering. The back room was a dark tangle of used frames, derelict wheels, seats, forks and various parts. It looked like a rat's nest, but Mr. Pullin could burrow into that thicket and, within moments and without exception, return with exactly the part the customer needed.

Setting our bikes on their kickstands out front, we entered Vern Pullin's ancient shop. First in the neat row of shiny two-wheelers was a clutch of Sting-Rays: red, green, blue, gold, every color imaginable. I ran my hand along the length of the white vinyl banana seat on a metal-flake burgundy "Ray" several times. Mr. Pullin stood behind the worn oak display counter, ages-old grease ringing his cracked and weathered fingers. He was flipping through a ledger of some sort and barely looked up. Apparently little boys frequenting his store, pining for the latest and greatest Schwinn, was nothing new to him. After a time, he asked: "Help you boys?"

"We . . . we . . . we wanna swing a trade for a couple of Sting-Rays."

Vern looked us up and down. "What cha got?"

We retreated to the sidewalk and began to wheel in our Racers. He stopped us. "Whoa, boys. Whoa. Them's two mighty nice machines you got there. I'll bet they was Christmas presents not too long ago."

"They were," we unisoned.

"Well," he said, scratching a gray stubble that looked permanent, "I'm not so sure Santee'd be too pleased if you was to give up a present he picked out special just for you."

"I'm too old to believe in Santee," I blurted, figuring it was far enough away from next Christmas for Santa to remember I might have said this.

Mr. Pullin dug at his chin a bit more. "Tell you what. I'll call your mama and let her know how much I can offer you in trade."

"But she doesn't . . ."

Raising an eyebrow, he turned to his ledger, leafed through a page or two and rattled off a phone number. "I'll call your mama." Unstated was *and that's final, boys.*

We pedaled home. Mom must have heard the crunching of our bicycle tires up the gravel drive. She dropped the laundry she was hanging out and met us before we could settle the Racers on their kickstands. The only part of the tirade I specifically recall was: "I'll not have you roaring through the neighborhood like some damned motorcycle gang member!"

~~~~~

Fifty-plus years later, somewhere out behind Beebo's house (on acreage similar to Mom and Dad's) there is a collection of old bicycles gathered from years of our riding and then our children riding. Deep in that pile of frames and wheels and rotted Brooks leather saddles, I suspect, one would find remnants of the old Schwinns. With a little bit of grease and Tri-flow and polish and care, I'd wager they'd be fit to ride again.

Should that happen, I know one of Santa's elves—an older one named Vern—will be viewing the scene, scratching his stubbly beard and smiling.

Paxton Hotel *1961*

FINALLY, WE WERE HEADING TO BUCKS LAKE. FOR AS long as I'd known him, Musty, the rich kid from down the street, talked about his cabin at Bucks Lake and how he could drink right out of a spring and dig for quartz crystals from a secret mine and swim in the lake and water ski behind a speed boat and stay up late at night.

Well, now we were on the road: Dad, Mom, Beebo and me. We were going to spend the weekend at Musty's cabin and do all of those wonderful things Musty'd been bragging about.

Bucks Lake is three hours from home up the windy Feather River Canyon. Although the canyon is ribboned with waterfalls, bedecked with slabs of glittering white granite and dotted with stands of oak and fir, three hours is a long ride. Especially when you're not yet 10 years old.

In the days before seatbelts, Beebo wanted to sit on my side of the car. Every turn in the road was his opportunity to slide further over and squish me. He also wanted my copy of *If I Ran the Zoo,* and he really wanted my Big Hunk candy bar because he'd already finished his.

"Mom..."

"That'll be about enough!" She'd said that more than once on this trip.

Dad never said a word. I sat directly behind him. I imagine he just gripped the steering wheel tighter and tighter and clenched his teeth the more we squabbled. But I'm not sure. All I could see was the back of his head and brother Beebo's big, fat...

~~~~~

We'd come about halfway, and we needed a break. Plus, Dad would be happy with a cold Lucky Lager.

A billboard said "Tavern—Ice Cold Beer—Fine Dining—Rooms" with an arrow. Dad wheeled off the highway and crossed a rusty steel bridge with wooden planking that spanned the river. A few hundred yards up from the bridge, in a flat area cut from the side of the hill, a rickety, two-story boarding house stood, next to a railroad line.

Dad pulled the station wagon to a stop and peered up through the windshield. I crawled over his shoulder to see what he was looking at.

The building looked like something out of *Bonanza* or *Tombstone Territory* with blistered paint on the walls and a hitching rail out front. A dozen or so steps climbed to a

The Old Hotel

decrepit porch. A gnarled rose twisted around a corner post and clung to the eaves of the veranda. The vine entwined itself around a faded sign reading Paxton Hotel.

Beebo climbed over me and tumbled out of the car. He wanted to be first and I was just the little brother. He darted up the stairs and I followed on his heels. Together we threw open the door and stopped. The sunlight from outside made a bright rectangle on the floor. Everything else was dark. The place smelled like the cellar at home and it took a minute for our eyes to adjust.

Dad pushed through us and found a place to order a beer.

The bar was at one end of a big, musty dance hall. I knew it was a dance hall because I watched *Gunsmoke* every Tuesday night. The room felt cold as a cavern. Along one wall stood an upright grand piano. I knew that the theme from *Wagon Train* could be played using only the black keys, and I sincerely wanted to prove this. I glanced back at Mom standing in that rectangle of sunlight, and she shook her head.

How did Mom always know what I was thinking?

A tattered woven rug covered a portion of the pocked wood floor. A gentle breeze slipped through the double-hung windows. Filmy, aged-to-yellow curtains danced in and out of the openings. An empty rocker was positioned to look out one of the windows, the one with the best view of the railroad track.

I edged toward it and slipped my fingertips along one arm.

"I wouldn't do that, boy." The voice was punctuated by a spasmy cough. The man who'd served up Dad's beer had come around the end of the bar. He was half the size of Dad with a tattered plaid shirt pulled over a round belly and partially tucked into filthy trousers. A stubby cigarette dangled from his gray lips.

I jerked my hand back.

"Boy," he said, "the woman who owned this old place, why, that was her chair."

I eyed the old wooden rocker. It was just an old wooden rocker.

"Yep, she and her husband built and ran this old hotel way before the turn of the century. Ever'thing's original, just like she left it."

I peered through the shadows. A table or two and a few wooden chairs were pushed against the wall just beyond the piano. A deer head hung above them, cobwebs threaded about its antlers. An American flag, suspended from its corners, drooped over a tiny, raised area at the far end of the room, its stars arranged differently from any American flag I'd ever seen.

The barkeep drew closer. I could smell the sooty stench of his cigarette. He gently put one hand on my shoulder and pointed down the tracks with the other one—the hand holding the smoke.

"One day, the old woman's husband—her one true love—why he hopped on that train to head down to Oroville to conduct some commerce of some sort or other. You know. Business."

I looked past the faded curtains, out the window and down at the railroad line that wound through the canyon and disappeared.

"Yep. The train pulled a whistle stop and let him on and off he went." The little man exhaled a bluish veil and coughed a deep, phlegmy cough. "Never come back."

"Never?" My voice squeaked wonder.

"Nope. Never did." He paused. "Old woman, why she positioned that rocker just exactly so and sat at that window mornin' 'til night, rockin' ever so gently. Waiting. Just waiting." A thoughtful pause and a slow exhale. "Waiting for her man to return."

My breath caught.

The barkeep took a final drag on his cigarette and snuffed it out in an old glass ashtray.

"One day, 'bout dusk, she was sittin' in that chair when a train come rumblin' up the canyon. Why you could hear them steam locomotives screamin', straining to pull a mile of box cars up the hill. By and by, it passed . . ."

I bit my lip and looked up at the man.

". . . and so did she."

I stepped away from the dead lady's chair.

"But you know what, sonny?" He gave a little squeeze to my shoulder. "'Round midnight, ever' night, when I come downstairs to kinda check things out and make sure the doors is all locked up, why, she's here—right there—rockin' in that chair. Ever so gently."

Another spasmy cough.

"I figure she's still waiting for her man, you know, her true love to return."

I turned to find Dad, but the little man clutched my upper arm and pulled me closer. He smelled like old socks.

"I seen her," he whispered.

His rancid breath made me wince and the moisture of his words sprayed the inside of my ear.

I tugged and wiggled away, needing to find Dad or Mom or even Beebo. Dad was finishing his beer at the bar. Mom was standing by the door, wishing we'd a get a move on. I found her skirts and clung to them.

The shaft of afternoon light still bathed the section of wood floor. I shot a glance over my shoulder toward the pot-bellied barkeep and squeezed Mom ever more tightly. A breeze wafted through and disturbed the yellowy curtains.

The proprietor had moved back behind the bar where he tapped a fresh cigarette on the counter. He coughed a bit and acted as if he needed to spit. "We've got rooms tonight." He laughed. "Spend the night, sonny boy. I'll wake you up and you c'n see her too."

The next thing I remember was sitting in the back seat of the car. I don't remember Mom frantically sweeping me into her arms or carrying me down the steps or depositing me in the back seat, although I'm certain she did these things.

For a while Beebo and I both sat in the back seat quiet. Real quiet. Then I saw he had used my sticky, half-eaten Big Hunk to bookmark a page in *If I Ran the Zoo,* and that made me mad. Just as I started to give Beebo what for, Dad glanced over his shoulder said, "You boys better pipe down or I'll turn around and leave you two back at that hotel." Then he laughed, while Mom counseled, "Clayton, just watch the road."

~~~~~

I'm not sure if we ever dug for crystals or went swimming that weekend at Musty's cabin on Bucks Lake. I know I never learned to water ski.

I also know I didn't want Dad to stop for a beer at the Paxton Hotel on the trip back home.

Bonfire of the Eight Year Olds *1961*

THE TREES IN THE ORCHARD OUT BACK WERE DYING. the cause was a mystery to Dad, who knew little of almond farming. The trees wore a thick black bark. On some, an occasional dollop of yellow resiny pitch oozed, impossible to clean out of trousers or shirts using Oxydol and nearly impossible to clean out of hair without a lot of turpentine. The pitchy barked trees were in the center of the grove. One spring, two of those pitchy trees didn't produce buds, blossoms or leaves. Dead, they stood naked in the midst of the old orchard. Dad bought a new Homelite chainsaw from the local hardware store, mixed up some oil and gas like he knew what he was doing, and cut the remains down. The suckers and brush he piled near where the trees had stood. The limbs and stumps he cut into 16-inch lengths for later use in the house's Franklin fireplace. Harvested wood. This was like living off the land.

A fungus appears when a valley oak is cleared out but the roots are left to rot in the ground. When the fungus attacks the roots of an almond or peach, the tree quickly dies. Call it karma in its most agricultural of forms. But Dad didn't know anything about karma or oak root fungus. All he knew was that the following year, three or four more trees didn't bud, the next year, several more. One by one, the dead trees had to be removed. In short order, a wide swath of our orchard was gone, and the woodpile for the Franklin stove had grown to a decades-long supply. Meanwhile, the brush pile in the middle of what used to be the grove became a neighborhood legend: a mecca for Nilley and Musty and the Calvies and friends I didn't know I had.

Better than the best jungle gym at the nearby elementary school, the pile of twigs and sticks was a hive of activity on Saturday afternoons. At first, we simply climbed to the heights of the pile and bounced up and down as if on some primitive trampoline. Then one day we decided to burrow into its mass, clearing sticks and suckers to create a path to its interior. We hollowed out a cavern and soon added passages to rooms here and there. Many times throughout the construction process, we learned that moving one too many limbs was like playing Pic-Up-Stix but on a much larger scale. More than once, the ceiling of our lodge would collapse and a half dozen or more kids would scramble and scratch their way to the perimeter of the pile. Someone began to sing the appropriate verse about a timber cracking at the bottom of the mine from Jimmy Dean's then-hit "Big John." Soon we started randomly pulling branches from the structure just so we'd have an excuse to sing the song, never concerned that this delayed the overall project. There would be plenty of Saturdays.

When the engineering and construction phase was complete, we moved in, hanging old clothes on stick stubs and hauling in raggedy blankets and camping cookware. We sat on the bare floor now packed hard by weeks of sneakered traffic and played Chinese checkers or Go Fish or pushed Tootsie-Toy cars and trucks through the dirt. Occasionally someone would bring Cragmont sodas and cookies or crackers, and we'd all have a meal in there. One evening, Beebo and the boys and I decided we'd grab our sleeping bags and camp out, pretending to be members of the local Mechoopda Indian tribe, living off the land like in olden days. But Mom caught us slipping out of the house with our bedrolls.

"Rats!" she implored. "Filthy rats and disgusting little field mice live in that wood pile. And raccoons! And all kinds of vermin!"

One of us looked at her and asked, "What's a vermin?"

"Never mind!" she raged. "You kids could contract the plague or something worse. Maybe even rabies!" punctuating that statement with: "And then what?"

She turned to Dad who was standing nearby probably suppressing a grin. She pointed at his chest and said, "Clayton! That pile has got to go!"

So one Saturday in November, after the first few good and soaking rains of the season, using our tunnel for access, Dad poured a little weed oil or kerosene or some other flammable accelerant into one or two rag-stuffed shoeboxes and pitched them in through the top of the pile into the middle of the heap. Hollering "Stand back!" he lit an entire book of matches and tossed them toward the makeshift wick. Missing, he lit a second. Then a third.

Feeling an urge to volunteer because I was a naturally helpful kid and I knew my way around in there, I said, "I can crawl in and . . ."

"No!" Dad exclaimed raising a hand to gesture me away, "You'll get hung up on somethin' and burn to a crisp. And I'd never hear the end of it." Then he shinnied in.

Seconds later, a flaming matchbook hit its mark. With an audible *whooooosh,* air from the immediate surroundings whistled past us toward the flame.

"Jumpin' Jehosophat!" Dad yelled. He didn't bother to crawl back out the tunnel; he just bulled his way through the thicket. Eyebrows singed and with his denim ranch jacket steaming, his grin was about as bright as the flames that, a few feet behind him, reached far into the heavens.

Within minutes, the rising sparks and column of black, oily smoke had attracted all of the kid–construction crew to the side of the rapidly diminishing brush pile. We formed a ring around the inferno and stood silently, each thinking separate thoughts about the fort/castle/mansion that was disintegrating in front of our very eyes. At some point, a kid picked up a stick from the margins of the blaze and, stepping forward, flicked it toward the middle. But the fire was so intense that he immediately stepped back. After a few moments, however, he tossed in another.

Before too many of us could join in this controlled practice of pyromania, Nilley told us: "Remember, if you all play with the fire, you'll likely wet the bed tonight. Least that's what my mama always told me." He waved an index finger at us convincingly, adding, "Mark my words."

All of us knew Nilley's mama a bit too well and understood that she was not a mother whose authority was to be questioned. We dropped whatever combustibles we had in our hands. No one wanted to take any chances.

Throughout the day and into the evening, Dad tended the blaze, turning the fuel on the fire's rim toward the middle, again, like he knew what he was doing. Against a gray November chill, we watched the pile crumble and fall in upon itself, envisioning wispy devils swirling and twisting and disappearing into the ever-changing red-orange recesses of the coals, relishing the heat they produced, turning our backs to the glow when our fronts got too warm and then turning round again. About dusk, Mom came to the group with a large bag of Stay Puft Campfire marshmallows, handing a few to each of my remaining colleagues one at a time, answering somebody's question like this: "Well, no, I don't suppose roasting marshmallows could be considered playing with the fire," she said. "Why do you ask?"

Mom must have been correct because the next day, when everybody reassembled to see what was left of the bonfire, I asked if anyone had wet the bed the night before. No one admitted to having done so.

Sugar Blues 1962

"MY BOYS WILL ALWAYS CARRY ONE OF THESE," DAD said as he handed me a tiny package on my 10th birthday. "It's very special."

I tore into the wrapping paper with bits flying all over the back patio and onto the frosting of the cake Mom had baked for me, much to her exasperation. Inside was a Hohner Marine Band harmonica in the key of C. I immediately placed it against my lips and began blowing. Blowing and sucking and blowing. Special, indeed. The perfect noisemaker for a 10-year-old. Beebo, who'd been given one a couple of years earlier, came running out of the house with his and joined in a raucous duet.

Mom quickly reached a boiling point, prompting Dad to raise his hands. "No, boys," he said, "it goes like this." Pulling his Hohner Chromonica—his bigger harmonica, one that could play sharps and flats—from a forepocket in his khakis, he tapped the thing three times against the palm of his hand. Then he launched into his rendition of Clyde McCoy's "Sugar Blues."

Dad played the "Sugar Blues" often. He and his Barstow High School buddy Ralphie Fairbanks perfected their version of it in about 1936. It may be the only melody he ever mastered on his mouth harp. He played it in the bathtub, where the acoustics were good. He played it around the campfire, impressing, he assumed, folks at nearby sites. Often, after watching Walter Cronkite, he'd pop open a beer, move out to the patio and serenade the neighborhood with his signature tune. It was either that or cuss at the TV.

~~~~

Dad's 1950 Willys Jeepster was not the most dependable vehicle of the era. He'd purchased it used in about 1965. It would be the family's first second car. Bright red with a black convertible top and fold and tumble access to a back seat, Dad's Jeepster was his conveyance to the rugged backcountry north and east of Chico. "Ishi's stompin' grounds," he called them. And many weekends he'd pile Beebo and me in the backseat and head east up a state highway out of Red Bluff to an unpaved fire trail called the Ponderosa Way. On that remote route we'd hang out at Bruff's Camp or Peligreen Place or the Cave at Kingsley Cove to "live like Ishi" for a day or two. And live like Ishi we did, although I always doubted that California's last wild Indian ever played "Sugar Blues" to his clan on a harmonica.

On the return from just such a trip, the Jeepster's aging Hurricane 4 engine sputtered and died. It was on Highway 36 west of Payne's Creek where we found ourselves coasting

Dad's Jeepster broke down again

powerless down and around a bend and coming to rest, luckily, in a gravel wide spot. Being the era 50 years before cell phones, Dad clambered out of the phaeton, figured out that there was still gas in the tank and, after a short time, waved down a passing motorist. They spent a few minutes looking under the hood and shrugging. Dad gave the stranger a dime, and he agreed to call Triple A once he got to a pay phone. In the meantime, all we could do was wait.

Dad settled back into the driver's seat and said, "Boys, this is why you always need to carry one of these." He reached into the glovebox to recover his big harmonica and began playing the "Sugar Blues."

It was only a few years before Dad's Jeepster died a quiet death. Towed one final time, it was replaced with something more reliable, something called a Land Cruiser from Japan.

Dad slipped his old Hohner into the glovebox, but never found cause to play it by the side of the road. Still, his mouth harp wouldn't be silenced.

On our countless trips to the back country, Dad would remind us that "the soundtrack of the West is played on one of these." Then, after tapping the Chromonica on his palm three times, he wouldn't mournfully play "Streets of Laredo" or "Red River Valley."

No. Whether serenading campers around the evening fire or sitting for a spell beside a mountain lake, it was always his impeccable version of the "Sugar Blues."

Occasionally, I'll dust off my harmonica and take a run at Dad's tune, but it was Dad's tune, and out of respect—or lack of ability—I give up and try to figure out a melody of my own.

Nilley's Bomb Shelter   1962

NILLEY'S DAD BUILT A BOMB SHELTER IN THEIR backyard. Here's why:

In 1962, as the Cold War was heating up, a group of New Yorkers wanting to leave what they presumed to be the Soviet Union's number 1 or number 2 US target, conducted a study to determine where the safest place in all of the United States might be. *En masse*, they'd relocate there. A small college town in California's northern Sacramento Valley topped the list, and soon a caravan of U-Hauls bearing the possessions of people who talked funny, according to Mom, paraded into Chico. Because of this population growth, not too much time passed before someone decided that our little town warranted a higher degree of national security, and so construction soon began on a Nike inter-ballistic missile base just north of the municipal airport. Shortly thereafter, Chico showed up on a Soviet map of possible/probable targets.

That was enough for Nilley's dad. "Gotta be safe from the God-damned Ruskies!" Mr. Vanella declared.

His real name was Jimmy, but we all had to call him Mr. Vanella. Mr. Vanella, his wife Margarite, and their two boys, Victor and Danny—whom we all called Nilley—had lived in the neighborhood long before our family moved in. They had a small gray stucco house that faced the creek on a triangular lot bordered on two sides by paved streets. The backyard had a small fruit orchard originally, but the trees didn't do well because Mr. Vanella overwatered them and one by one, they all died.

"We'll put it out where the orchard used to be," Mr. Vanella said. "The boys and me can dig the hole. Maybe some neighbor kids can help."

We didn't.

~~~~

Jimmy Vanella worked for the local utility as an electrical engineer. The inside of his garage was always cluttered with wires and gadgets most of us kids marveled at but could not understand. There wasn't room for the big green and white Buick station wagon that Margarite Vanella used to ferry Nilley to his private school and Victor to the special class he had to attend. A group of us boys would visit Nilley's dead orchard from time to time, but there was nothing much to do back there and Nilley seemed happier when he was with us and we were somewhere else.

Like just about everything when you're a kid, construction of the bomb shelter seemed to take forever. Mr. Vanella picked and shoveled and dug the loamy soil from his back

> "... the clear water turned muddy and swept Nilley's backyard away a few cubic feet at a time."

forty, loaded it into a garden wheelbarrow and pushed it from his yard, across the road to the banks of Chico Creek where he'd dump the thing. We'd watch as the clear water turned muddy and swept Nilley's backyard away a few cubic feet at a time. One day a big cement mixer truck stopped in the middle of Stewart Avenue, and we all gathered to watch as its load poured into forms crafted by Mr. Vanella. The big truck visited several times that day, and while it was gone, we could hear Jimmy Vanella scraping the wet concrete and barking commands at Danny and Victor, ultimately telling Victor to get out of the hole, saying, "I'll just have to do it myself."

Nilley should have been so fortunate.

~~~~~

Sometime between the conception of Nilley's bomb shelter and its completion, I, as a 10-year-old, pulled a copy of John Hersey's *Hiroshima* from Dad's bookshelf. I wanted to know what an atom bomb would do. (Published in 1959 as a Bantam 35 cent paperback, I still have the book in my collection.) I recall the horror I couldn't put down as I waded through the text. I recall images of a blinding flash and of eyes melting out the sockets of people still standing. Of buildings turned to dust. Of fire. I recall several nights of crawling into Mom and Dad's tiny double bed, unable to sleep by myself.

~~~~

"Where have you boys been?" Mom asked that afternoon.

"Watchin' 'em pour CEEment over at Nilley's bomb shelter."

"Oh my God," she said. "If the Russians ever bomb this place, can you imagine what it will be like when that old coot Jimmy Vanella comes out of that damned fallout shelter? It's going to be a damned desert!"

"A radioactive one at that," Dad added.

I knew Mom and Dad were right. I pictured dust. I pictured fire. I pictured a hazy, gray wind blowing over a dry, scorched, leveled neighborhood. I would probably be unable to sleep by myself tonight.

Then Mom added: "Everything was fine until those damned New Yorkers showed up."

~~~~

Eventually, the thing was done. Mr. Vanella admonished all of us neighborhood boys that we were unwelcome because we didn't help when we had the chance.

"Wanna check it out?" Nilley asked a bunch of us one afternoon.

Nilley knew his dad's rule, but he also knew his dad's work schedule pretty well, and he had a Timex wristwatch.

"Well, sure," we all agreed.

A brick-red steel storm door slanting out of the weeds and dirt was all that showed on the floor of the derelict orchard. Although brand new, the hinges sang and squeaked as Nilley butterflied them open. He reached down and flipped a switch. Bare lightbulbs glowed at the top and the bottom of the steep metal staircase painted the same color as the storm door. Our footfalls echoed as we clambered down each tread. At the bottom, another steel door, although a regular one. Nilley hit a switch there and opened up.

The interior was of unfinished concrete. It still smelled wet. A cooking area and a tiny bathroom with the toilet in the shower stall were placed at the far end. Floor-to-ceiling cabinets—nice solid ones—lined opposite sides of the great room.

"For food and games and Dad's short wave," Nilley said.

He opened a cabinet. Canned beans and vegetables, a stack of canned Spam and some Vienna sausages were neatly arranged on shelves. Some cloth sacks of flour and sugar lay on another shelf. Inside another section: canteens of water and bottles of Nehis and Coca-Cola. On the top shelf of that cabinet was a wicker basket. Nilley dragged a small stepladder over and pulled the basket down. Snickers bars, Milky Ways, Butterfingers, peanuts, chips, Red Vines. It was a bonanza.

"Just take one," Nilley warned.

In the cabinets along the opposite walls was a cache of games—Monopoly, Password, chess/checkers, Yahtzee and a few others as well as Nilley's treasured Lionel train set. "I'll get to set it up down here any time I want until . . ." Nilley stopped. "Until . . ."

Nilley didn't need to say what the hideout was really for. We all knew.

～～～

Though stark, the bomb shelter appeared to be a fine rumpus room to all of us who crowded in that first day. During regular but short stretches between when we all arrived home from our schools and Nilley's dad returned from work, we did rumpus there quite often, raiding the snack basket and setting up Nilley's train and building forts out of blankets and stuff. One time Calvie tried smoking cigarettes, but the smoke had nowhere to go, and we all ended up racing up the stairs, gasping for clean air. Fortunately, Mr. Vanella rarely visited the fallout shelter once Mrs. V. took off. So the smoke had time to dissipate, and he never found out about the little tryst with the Marlboros, and we got to where we never bothered to replenish the depleted snack basket.

By the time we reached high school, we'd found other things to interest us, and the thought of climbing down into that dank and musty fallout shelter held less and less appeal.

～～～

Nilley's dad and mom divorced. It was the first time that had happened in the neighborhood. Nobody ever figured out where Margarite ran off to in her big Buick, but one day she was simply gone. Jimmy Vanella was left to raise Danny and Victor. About 10 years later, shortly after Nilley and I graduated from high school, Mr. Vanella up and died unexpectedly.

"The old coot probably had a stroke," Mom said.

Nilley, taking a page from his father's book, studied electrical engineering, got himself married, and went off to work in Washington, DC. He never looked back.

The house Nilley grew up in sold long ago and the new owners converted the bomb shelter into a swimming pool. One with substantial cabinets for storage, I suppose.

And for years Victor could be seen waving at people while riding a white, fat-tired bicycle around town. Everybody knew him by name, including the newcomers from New York.

Mom's Manzanita Tea 1963

MOST KIDS GROWING UP NEAR OUR BRANCH OF CHICO Creek came home with flaming cases of poison oak several times from spring through fall. A bubbly, itching, burning rash started somewhere on a bare ankle or elbow that had contacted the oily, reddish-green leaves of a bush that bordered creeks and trails in our area. I'd get tangled up in it regularly, and because, at seven or eight years old, I couldn't discipline myself not to scratch the itch, the stuff would spread across my body, onto my face, into my eyes. And woe be unto me if "nature should call" after I'd inadvertently made hand-to-shrub contact with the evil plant. Invariably, a trip to Doctor Lott's office would follow, one that included a rather embarrassing exam followed by a shot of something for the itch, a shot that was only slightly less unpleasant than the rash.

Franny Wildermire, the earthiest mother in the neighborhood, knew of a potion that would make almost anyone almost immune from poison oak's ravages.

Mom's Manzanita Tea

"Manzanita tea," Franny insisted.

Frustrated with my brother Beebo and me being brought to itchy red tears so frequently, our mother said, "We're gonna try it!"

So one early spring afternoon, we ventured to the bluff side of Bidwell Park charged with the mission of returning home with a paper sack full of waxy leaves from the smooth, red-barked manzanitas that grew in the rocky, sunbaked soil up that way.

Deftly, Mom spread our quarry on a glass table out on the patio to dry as she supposed tea leaves dried. When the time was right—moms know when the time is right—she set a pot to boiling on the stove and crumbled the now-brittle leaves into the caldron. The kitchen soon smelled of a vapor we'd never previously . . . umm . . . experienced. Mom, who'd somehow lost her sense of smell back when she was a little girl, stood stirring the pot and singing an off-key version of "Swingin' on a Star."

Beebo and I retreated to the patio.

Forty-five minutes—maybe an hour—later, she appeared at the back door with two steaming teacups. Making one of those mom offers no kid is allowed to refuse, she handed Beebo and me a cup. I ran mine under my nose. If someone had tossed their creek-damp cutoffs in the corner of the closet instead of in the laundry basket or, better yet, if someone accidentally wet their pants and was so embarrassed that they tossed their soiled undies to molder in the corner of the closet for a week rather than use the hamper—not that I have personal experience in this regard—that's how bad this concoction smelled. Maybe worse.

"Drink up, you two," Mom said with a satisfied grin. "Franny says if you drink some of this a couple of times a week, you'll never have to worry about getting poison oak ever again."

I took a sip. Outside of the time I put a drop of Bactine on my tongue just to see what it'd taste like, this would be my first experience with bitter. My eyes began to water, but my mouth couldn't. I wanted to spit out the aftertaste but couldn't even muster cotton. I'm not sure if my throat constricted, but it should have. Beebo and I were smart enough not to comment or complain to our proud mama over her efforts, but Dad, who'd been "asked" to join in this medicinal endeavor, suggested it might be better with a sweetener. We quickly discovered that no amount of honey or 7-Up or molasses or even Jack Daniels would make the potion easier to swallow, although Dad seemed okay with his and a finger or two of Jack.

For the next few weeks, as a family, we began choking down Mom's Manzanita Tea. Awful as these tasting events were, the good news was this: I was immune: *Immune from the ravages and rashes of poison oak!* So was Beebo. We brushed against it with our bare legs. We waded through it to get to the creek, even used its oily stalk to pull ourselves out of the water. And we laughed at the rest of the neighborhood boys who pussy-footed around the shrub.

"Chickens!" we'd point and yuk. "Ya big chickens!"

Immunity was a great thing—a freeing thing. Or so we'd thought. Within about a month, the worst, most highly inflamed, itchiest, nastiest-red-rashiest case of poison oak Beebo and I'd ever come down with landed us in Dr. Lott's waiting room—and almost the hospital.

FIRST DAY OF SPRING—A HALF-CENTURY LATER: I joined a naturalist-led tour of the Bishop's Ranch retreat a few miles west of Healdsburg. Along with 20 other hikers touring riparian habitats and oak-studded pastureland and swales, we learned about the unique features of the California salamander, the secrets hidden within an oak gall, the bizarre

Manzanita's "little apples"

life cycle of the turret spider and how to spot her den, and this: "California's 'First People' used to make a Manzanita Tea."

My ears perked up.

"*Manza* means 'apple' and *ita*, of course, 'little.' Little apple," our guide explained. "In the spring, the Manzanita bush will produce a lovely white flower which, in the autumn, will develop into a little apple. The local natives would pick the tiny apples and set them out to dry. Then they'd grind the apple into a powder and place the powder in boiling water to steep."

Apparently, this little apple step—the step actually involving fruit—was something earthy ol' Franny Wildermire failed to share some 60 years prior. That, or Mom failed to hear.

For the rest of the Bishop Ranch outing, I wondered if this ancient beverage rendered any local First People anywhere on the planet immune from the fiery rash poison oak offered. But I didn't ask.

I also didn't ask, "Did they do anything with the leaves?"

The Day My Teacher Cried *1963*

ON THE DAY THE TEACHER CRIED, WE HAD JUST COME in from morning recess.

Our teacher, Mr. Kaywoody, was not a funny man. Or particularly likable, for that matter. Maybe he thought he was still in the Army Air Corps or something. Or maybe that's just how you dealt with 34 preteens in a classroom. Outside of his odd name, there was little that my cohort of sixth graders laughed about or enjoyed that I could remember, other than we could address him as Mr. Kay if we wanted to. Slender as a fencepost, he wore sharply creased pants, a crisp white shirt and a skinny tie drawn tightly up to his Adam's apple. His slip-on shoes had tassels and a reflective shine. He seated us in strict rows and columns as if we were simply a chart filled with kids. There would be no groupings of seats, and no one could get out of his or her seat without first raising a hand and asking. And it better not be to go to the lavatory. Mr. Kay's responses to questions or comments always seemed clipped and short, buttoned-down and businesslike. "You'll be going to junior high next year," he said more than once. "There'll be no time for falderal there. They just won't put up with it."

So neither did he.

Morning recess was a welcome time for all of us to exhale and unwind. Nilley and the Calvert boys and Musty and me would start that break with a game of flag football and generally ended up on the bench because somebody tackled somebody else. From there we'd watch the littler kids play four-square or tetherball or we'd spy on the girls as they jumped rope. As sixth-grade boys, watching girls jump rope had somehow become more entertaining than it had been in previous years.

Particularly when it came to Rebecca Langworthy. Becca sat one row ahead and one column to the right of me in class. Things were happening to her that were happening to a few of the other girls, but certainly nothing like that was happening to any of the boys in my class yet, except for John Prince, who'd flunked twice. From my vantage point, I was captivated by various, mysterious curves, especially those pressed against the cold steel and wood seat of her desk. During silent reading I'd ignore whatever book was in my hands and wistfully dream of slipping my fingers through the flowing curls of her red hair while sharing a Hires or a Dad's Root Beer with two straws in a field of wild daisies.

Not that I'd ever spoken to her. *Gawd no! Never!*

But on those rare occasions when I hadn't been benched, I would elbow my way to the front of the boys' line, hustle to my seat and inhale a little more deeply as she passed by to hers.

On the day the teacher cried, we had just come in from recess. I was thinking thoughts of Rebecca Langworthy, noting her red hair and, considering my own, wondered if our children might be redheads. Lifting my eyes from her in her lovely autumn plaid jumper, I noticed that Mr. Kay was facing the chalkboard. He hadn't turned around. I also realized that my classmates' chatter had subsided and they'd settled in more quickly than usual. Or was I just more mesmerized by Becca than normal?

It was arithmetic period. Usually, Mr. Kay would chalk a problem on the board and then wander through the rows and columns of his pupils, checking to see if we had remembered yesterday's lesson. But this day he wasn't writing a problem on the board. Instead, his hand was lifted, pinching the stick of chalk, but it wasn't moving. He seemed frozen. Something was haywire. I'd never heard the classroom so silent for so long. I held my breath, along with Nilley and Musty and the others, and saw a few kids glancing from side to side. I glanced around also, being careful not to look Rebecca Langworthy's way. I'm not sure why.

That silent eternity ended when Mr. Kaywoody lowered his hand, the one holding the chalk—was it trembling?—and turned to face us. He scanned the room, perhaps making eye contact with each of his students, then he dropped his gaze to the floor. What came next was nearly inaudible: "Boys and girls, what we know right now is that the President is dead."

Immediately, the silence became deeper, thicker. It seemed as if all the air had left the room.

Mr. Kay turned back to the board and placed the chalk in the tray. I saw his shoulders shudder. Everyone probably did. Facing the board, he said, "Mr. Eldrid [our school principal] tells me you'll all be going home to be with your folks right away." Then there was more of that silent eternity.

During those cold minutes, my 11-year-old thinking rendered this queer thought: "There's God, there's Jesus, there's the President of the United States and then there's Walt Disney. What should happen if something would happen to any one of these?" I figured I was about to find out.

Image of a sad, sad day (CBS News archive image)

Soon Mr. Eldrid came on the intercom and made the announcement: We were to go home. Mr. Kay stood by the door as we quietly filed out, and he did something he'd never done before. He hugged each one of us. I believe I even felt a tear graze my cheek. It was warm.

Over the next few days there was only classical music on the radio and even on the TV most of the time. News coverage on our black-and-white RCA Victor interrupted the symphonies and chorales, and at one point I saw somebody shoot somebody else in the gut in a basement somewhere. Mom immediately switched off the television and told us to go outside. The Calvert boys came over, but we didn't play. I'm not even sure we talked.

A week or so later, when classes resumed, we filed into our seats. For an instant, one row ahead and one column to the right, Rebecca Langworthy looked over her shoulder and right at me. I don't know why she did this.

Mr. Kay stood at the front of the room in his pressed pants, starched shirt and skinny tie and took roll. No mention was made of the assassination of President Kennedy. We simply opened our spellers to unit 14 and began to study the list of words for that week.

Honey Run Bridge   1964

BOB COOKE'S '65 PICKUP DIDN'T HAVE PLATES YET. BOB Cooke's kid was crazy. And the Honey Run Bridge was a historic landmark.

My family's orchard backed up to the Cooke place. I'd walk to school through the groves of trees with a neighbor girl named Angie who was a few years older than me. She'd tell me about high school life and which teachers to look out for in junior high. If I'd have had an older sister, I like to think she'd have been just like Angie. In the fall, the ground was dusty, littered with fallen leaves and the occasional derelict almond. In the spring, the air was fragrant with the aroma of the farming world's sweetest blossoms. Or was that aroma Angie? The ground, shaded under a canopy of fresh leaves, was wet those spring mornings, particularly as the weeds and wild grasses grew tall. That is, unless Dad and old man Cooke had knocked those weeds down with their disk plows and spring tooth harrows like they did every month or so.

I remember watching Mr. Cooke operate his fancy big Ford Ferguson. His tractor was newer than ours, with headlights and a big soft seat and switches and safety stuff our vintage '47 didn't have. At some point he disconnected the deadman switch from beneath that big, padded seat so, while wearing his cap at a cocky angle, he could set the tractor in low, low gear, hop off, walk beside it and talk to whomever might be near by—like Angie or me or his kid—while the thing dragged a disk through the dark, loamy orchard floor. At the end of a row, he'd step back on, lift the disk, turn to the next row, set the throttle and hop off again. I pictured him landing wrong or stumbling and getting crushed under the big Ford's water-filled rear tires. It never happened. Still, it seemed crazy to me.

So I guess crazy came natural to Bob's kid.

I don't think Angie saw things that way. There came a time when her *isn't-my-l'il-buddy-cute?* toward me gave way to a mooney-eyed something-er-other directed toward the Cooke kid, which I failed to understand. Once, on the way home from school just after the September harvest when a few missed nuts lay on the orchard floor, I came across Angie and the kid out past the burn pile.

Angie showed me a handful of almonds still in the hull. "We're pickin' up culls."

The kid glared at me. "So get lost, squirt."

"Yeah. Get lost," Angie said, but she didn't look at me when she said it.

I didn't like Bob Cooke's kid.

Bob Cooke and my father drank Brown Derby beer.

"Cheap stuff, son," Dad would say after spending a couple of hours on the tractor, "but perfect for washing the dirt and crud out of your mouth after a day's work."

I know for a fact that Bob and Dad shared a few Derbies more frequently than the knock-down-the-weeds schedule that they maintained. Walking home from school after practice, I'd come across them sitting on camp chairs in the shade of the almonds amidst a circle of empties. Dad, the letter carrier, talked about his aching feet, barking dogs on his route that should know him by now, and the number of worthless flats in the day's mail.

Bob, a butcher at a Safeway store, often mentioned another close call. "Damned near cut off another digit today," he'd say with a grin, waving his three-fingered left hand.

One afternoon, as I crossed the orchards wading through weeds and grasses, Bob said, "Clayton . . . I mean your dad here . . . we're havin' a beer. Want one?" He hoisted a stubby, brown bottle in my direction.

I said okay and took a tentative sip. It tasted like skunk water as near as I could tell. I tried to hand it back to him.

"C'mon kid, have a real drink."

Dad raised his hand. "Son, it's okay to say no."

"Say no? When's he gonna start growin' up?"

Dad took the bottle from me and handed it to Cooke. "He's barely 12, Cookie."

Bob Cooke dropped the bottle on the orchard floor. As I bent down to pick it up, he motioned me away. Then he shattered the bottle with the heel of his shoe.

Old man Cooke seemed crazy to me. I think Dad thought so too sometimes.

~~~~

Honey Run Road, a twisty stretch of dilapidated pavement, once was the main route between Chico, on the valley floor, and Paradise, Gold Rush–era settlement set at the edge of the yellow pine belt. Steep and chiseled into Butte Creek's canyon wall, the route formerly carried goods and mail and sightseers on buckboards and stagecoaches up the hill and away from the valley's frigid winter tule fog and stifling summer heat. The Honey Run Covered Bridge, built in 1887, offered an all-weather crossing of the creek.

The waters flowing beneath the span teemed with trout and salmon; the banks served as cover for beaver lodges and refuge for families of mallards and wood ducks. Overarching black oaks, springtime wildflowers, squawking jays, rattling woodpeckers and grazing mule deer made the crossing more than just a bridge. My family often packed sandwiches and sodas and pedaled our Schwinn three-speeds the dozen miles from home into the canyon and to the Covered Bridge. On special days, Angie would tag along.

From a distance, the graying wood edifice looked like a skinny barn with a creek running under it. The structure was only wide enough to accommodate one car or truck at

Honey Run Covered Bridge

a time. It was supported by 80-year-old timbers set upon ancient concrete footings. The deck, once rough-hewn four-inch-thick planking, was worn smooth and slightly rutted from decades of use. Vertical boards nailed to the wooden truss weathered and cracked over time. The whole structure groaned and creaked under the weight of any passing vehicle, and the kicked-up dust took minutes to settle. Shards of daylight, filtering through cracks in the wooden walls and shingled roof, danced on the dust in the air.

To be inside was to travel back in time. On one visit, Angie and I pedaled our bikes across and back, across and back, in long narrow ovals, until she got bored or saddle sore or something and headed off to wade in the creek or watch the ducks. I continued: round and round, smelling the musty dust and listening to the soft chorus of water flowing below, its melody joined by the echoes of clattering hooves, squealing grease-starved wooden axles and whistles and yips of the teamster. I imagined myself a 49er, waving at a passing freight wagon as I led my burro, lashed with grub and kit, to some remote claim upstream where I'd strike it rich—until Angie, standing backlit at one end of the bridge barn, hollered: "Your mom says it's time to quit."

I was content to keep riding and make it to my claim.

"She thinks you won't have the poop to ride all the way home." Then she chuckled.

"Mom!" I hollered back, "Angie said poop."

Mom stepped out of the shadows, thrust a sandwich my way and said, "No. *I* said poop. Now eat."

While wading in the waters in the shadow of the bridge, my pal Angie and I ate.

~

As Paradise grew, a bigger, wider and faster highway was constructed atop the ridge to the south. Fewer vehicles—mainly sightseers and residents—used the old bridge and the

> " . . . rocketing down the road's narrow corkscrews, hoping that my three-speed's brakes wouldn't give out . . . "

Honey Run. Because it was safer, Mom and Dad let me pedal my Schwinn up there anytime I wanted. More than once I chugged across the old bridge and grunted up the twisty, cliffside Honey Run all the way to Paradise. The payoff would be rocketing down the road's narrow corkscrews with preteen abandon, hoping that my three-speed's brakes wouldn't give out and toss me into the downslope thickets of stinging nettles and poison oak.

Less traffic also meant that on Friday and Saturday nights, because sheriff patrols busied themselves on the new road, it was safer for a kid and his girl to cruise up the Honey Run with a six-pack of whatever someone's dad wouldn't miss, find a wide spot with a distant view of Chico's twinkling lights, and prospect for something the lonely miners of the 1850s probably longed for more urgently than gold.

I'll always suspect the kid had told Bob he just wanted to show Angie the new pickup. And Bob being Bob said okay.

About halfway through the *Dick Van Dyke Show*, someone pounded on the back door. "Ah, nuts!" Dad said. "Who the hell could that be?"

Bob Cooke stood on the stoop, shaking. "Clayton, I . . . I need to borrow your car."

"You're in no condition. I'll drive."

I don't actually know what happened. I figure that the kid realized someone's curfew had been violated. Or maybe Angie rebuffed his advances. That's what I really hoped. Anyway, stoked by too many beers and harboring some frustration about opportunity lost and his healthy, young manliness going to waste, the kid raced his dad's new truck down the winding grade, tires chattering over broken pavement, squealing in and out of turns, headlights catching glimpses of canyon side, then space, then the wooden abutment of the Honey Run Covered Bridge.

The top-of-fold headline in the Saturday afternoon paper blared "Historic Bridge Destroyed!" The picture of the collapsed and splintered east end filled half the page. A full third of the span was gone, shingled roof, planked decking, everything. A portion of a crumpled pickup was wedged into the rubble and rock in the bed of Butte Creek. The paper reported that the cops found the kid sitting on a boulder on the east bank, banged up, bruised and disoriented. He was treated and later released.

The next day, they found Angie about a mile and a half downstream, submerged in a pool, pinned against the open outlet gate of a diversion dam. A couple of bottles of Brown Derby bobbed on the surface.

Honey Run Bridge

I never saw the kid again. I don't know where he went. Or where they sent him. The untended weeds grew tall in the Cooke orchard, and one day, Bob Cooke sold out to a developer. Soon we did too.

There was much talk about the Honey Run Covered Bridge. The collision shook the remaining portion from its timbered foundation. Canasta groups, history buffs, bar flies, college professors and county fathers all weighed in on what to do. A second concrete and steel bridge would be constructed just upstream "strong enough to support a fire engine and a water tender," as area property owners demanded.

Eventually volunteers from the local historical society saw to it that the old span was restored. Much of the material was salvaged from the wreckage, but some of the timbers and planks were new. In time, all would look old again.

The new covered bridge stood for another 50 years. But one November, the deadly wildfire that blew through the town of Paradise raced down the old road and into the canyon, incinerating the Honey Run Covered Bridge in a matter of seconds.

Recently, I borrowed a bicycle and pedaled up to the site. Spindly, blackened limbs of the few remaining oaks reached over the stream like wicked recollections, but the ground was carpeted in new winter grass and poppies. From the bank of Butte Creek, I watched a family of mallards paddle against the current and take refuge in an eddy on the other side. At my feet, water danced around a concrete footing that now footed nothing. As the water slipped past, I took a bit of comfort in its familiar, soft chorus.

Standing there, at least for a few moments, I found a refuge of my own—one with Angie.

Chesterfield Straights 1965

MY GRANDFATHER, "HAP" BAGNELL, SMOKED LUCKY Strikes, a habit conferred upon him by the US Army during World War I. So-called tailor-mades were once offered as part of a doughboy's C-rations. Young teens in the 1960s didn't receive C-rations, but we could easily get our hands on cigarettes. Cigarettes made us cool. Cigarettes made us adult. Cigarettes made the girls like us. Or so we thought.

In those days the Marlboro ad campaign was moving from the elegant choice for women of the forties and fifties to the rugged "come to where the flavor is" West. Cue Elmer Bernstein. Many of the guys in the seventh and eighth grade fancied themselves leather-skinned cow busters; therefore, the routes spoking out to the neighborhoods from the junior high were littered with Marlboro butts. Some kids were a bit more individualistic. Ernie, whose dad worked at the hardware store, lived a half mile away from me. He picked a menthol brand called Alpine. Their slogan was "Go to the mountains, it'll do a lot for you." Calvie was different too. His brand was Tareyton—

"I'd rather fight than switch"—which was fitting because he was a bit of a fighter, and, as things would turn out, he'd need to be. Ultimately, as kids were joshing and poking at each other and puffing on the way home from school, I felt late to the party. Out of the gang. Different, in a bad way. That's how you feel when you're 13. And I knew I needed to do something about it.

～～～

Out through a couple of orchards in back of our house, a tilt-up, pre-McDonald's hamburger stand was positioned next to the state highway. Going to the Jolly Kone was a slightly longer, alternate route from school, but there you could get an order of fries and a milkshake for about 85 cents, so a visit was worth the extra time and trouble. In the back corner of the stand's small, enclosed dining area stood a cigarette vending machine about the size of a jukebox. On the front of the machine were three or four rows of rectangular clear plastic buttons. Beneath each surface was a small likeness of a package of cigarettes. There must have been three dozen to choose from. Staring at it one day, while downing a strawberry shake and waiting for my fries to cool off, I was overwhelmed by all the choices. Which of these brands would ultimately be mine?

I wanted to fit in, so I had to start packin' smokes, but within limits, I liked being a bit different. So I eliminated Marlboro for obvious reasons and both Tareytons and Alpines. I considered Lucky Strikes for a long while but figured maybe I wasn't being fair with the other brands on that machine. I ruminated on this for quite some time until, walking home with the boys one day, I settled on a plan. I'd start with whatever brand was in the upper left-hand corner of those rows of buttons and move across until I settled on something that I liked. The next time I dropped in for my fries and shake, I figured I'd take the 15 cents change I was to get from my dollar bill, drop it in the slot, push that first button and pocket whatever came out.

One problem with this plan however: a pack of cigarettes cost 35 cents.

The next time, I'd be ready.

~~~

And I was.

I placed my order. "Hey. How's school today?" the white-clad man at the counter asked. "Your usual?" He knew me. He was the owner, the cashier and the cook.

"Yeah," I stammered as he slid my change across the Formica counter.

When he turned and went to work dropping my fries into the sizzling vat and whirring my shake together in the Hamilton Beach, I slipped over to the cigarette machine. The mechanical activity in the kitchen would certainly cover the sounds of my sin. Deftly I slipped a quarter I'd saved and the dime I'd just received into the slot. They clattered into place sounding like thunder to me. Knowing I didn't do *wrong* well, I glanced over my shoulder, happy to see the cook not peeking round the corner at me. I stabbed at the upper-left button.

Something tumbled out of the machine like a rock fall and thumped into a slot at the bottom. Blindly, I grabbed whatever had fallen out, slipped it into the front pocket of my jeans and escaped through the screened back door of the dining area. I'd be having no fries or shake this day.

Heart pounding, I raced through the orchards to an old shed I'd predetermined would be safe to begin my exploration of finer tobacco products and where I'd hidden a book of Hap's matches. Making the boy-cave, I paused for a moment to catch my breath. Then I fished in my pocket and pulled out the pack of cigarettes. Chesterfields. Never heard of 'em before. The package was adorned with some sort of shield or coat of arms and lettered in fancy English-style stuff.

Pretty sophisticated, I thought. I think I'm gonna like these!

I fumbled with the package until I found the slip of cellophane that when pulled would unwrap itself, revealing a foil top that I tickled open with my nervous fingers. Tightly packed inside was an unknown quantity of something tobacco-y enveloped neatly and uniformly in rolls of thin white paper. I picked and pulled and picked and pulled at one until, with a ragged end and its contents spilling out, the first cigarette came free. Mangled, I looked at the thing. I must have really torn it up because, unlike the Marlboros, Tareytons or Alpines, this one had no filter. It must have busted off, remaining in the package. I tossed the cigarette away, vowing to be more careful the next time. The second one came more freely from the pack. Its contents still tight and neatly wrapped,

> **"Maybe it's something you just have to get used to, so I took another drag."**

there was no filter on this one either. I peered into the dark cavity left by the first two samples but saw nothing. The third one came out with ease and, yet again, filterless.

Finally, I reasoned that this must be how this Chesterfields were made. Convenient, I thought, and you can light either end. So I picked one, stuck an end in my mouth and on about the third or fifth try, lit the other end.

If you could somehow combine week-old barbecue ash from our grill, wilted spinach dried and dotted blue with mold and, perhaps, some rusted steel wool, that flavor combination would fall well short of how awful what I'd just tasted, tasted. I pulled the thing out as my eyes began to water slightly. Maybe it's something you just have to get used to, I thought, so I took another drag. And then a third. Not good, but maybe getting better? What did I have to compare this taste to? For several minutes, I puffed and wiped my eyes and puffed and wiped my now dampening brow until the thing was burned down close enough to scorch my tender fingers.

Before I stubbed it out, I recalled that several of the boys could light a second one off the first if they held the new one steadily between their lips and touched the lighted tip of the nearly spent butt to it. And I'd seen Bogey do this in the movies. Cross-eyed, I tried it rather clumsily. In the process, the orange cinder of my first smoke briefly seared my thumb and index finger as I touched it to a replacement that wouldn't hold still in my unpracticed lips. Grimacing, I held on, thinking that this, perhaps, was something the Marlboro man had likely mastered. Maybe this contributed to his being so rugged and worldly and leathery. Less than halfway through the second, however, my forehead drenched, my body somehow sweaty, a chill hit me. I shivered a bit, then shook. I leaned back, then forward and heaved a painful dry heave. I was in way over my head.

Struggling to find my feet, I staggered from my hideout toward the house. Grandpa Hap intercepted me. "So, boy," he said, "How you like smokin' tailor-mades?"

I looked up at him though my watery eyes. *How the hell do adults always seem to know?* My lips quivered, but nothing came out.

"It'd be a good idea not to start," he said, winking and slapping me on the back.

And I didn't.

The next day I buried the rest of that pack of Chesterfields in the bottom of the garbage can—surely no one would find them there—and waited restlessly until the following Tuesday when the disposal company came by to cart off our trash.

~~~

When you're 13, 14 or 15, walking and poking and joshing your way to or from junior high, 60 seems old—a long time away. Suddenly, when you're in your sixties, it somehow seems young. Too young.

I think this as I am taking the long, slow journey home from services for my pal Calvie. Calvie, the kid who could shinny 40 feet up a sycamore to hang a rope swing; Calvie, who threw a wicked horseapple with pinpoint accuracy; Calvie, brave and quick enough to reach into murky creek water and catch racing crawdads without getting pinched.

"It was a tough year and a half," his sister told me, "but Calvie was a fighter." My pal Calvie.

A half-empty pack of Tareytons was found on the bedside table when he died.

The Art of Racing in November *1966*

TO CULMINATE A FOUR-WEEK PHYS-ED INSTRUCTIONAL unit on track and field, coach Johnny Carlisle planned an impromptu track meet. Kids were taught how to crouch at the start of a race, how to clear hurdles, how to put the shot, how to long jump and high jump and loads of other skills I knew I'd never use.

"Competitive competence," Coach C barked. "You guys that practice and get good might wanna join the track team come spring," he said, looking right past me.

Johnny Carlisle was a wiry redhead with a temper that always seemed to be on the verge of bubbling over. He acted the tough guy—perhaps it was all just a show—but I didn't much like him. I didn't think he liked me, either.

―――

My event was the 75-yard dash. Why just 75 yards? The schoolyard wasn't 100 yards wide.

Coach C paired me against Benjamin Dentz, a husky farm boy who lived out by the river. I sat a row behind Benny in social studies class and noticed that the backsides of his ears were never clean. Neither were his jeans.

"I'm gonna whup your ass," Benny snarled as we lined up at the heavy garden hose that served as the starting line.

Benny had at least 30 pounds on me, all muscle, I was sure, because I heard he could horse 90-pound sacks of nitrogen fertilizer into the back of his pop's Studebaker pickup and that he got to drive a Jeep through the orchards on their property out by the river whenever he wanted.

I, on the other hand, had never made it to the top of the 15-foot rope we were all supposed to climb in the gym for fitness tests every quarter. "Zero again?" Coach C would groan as I dropped from the rope. I couldn't muster a pull-up, either. I was just a skinny junior high kid who'd outgrown his pants' inseams. A beanpole. A weakling.

And Benny knew it. I figured he probably *would* whup my ass.

~~~~

I stood dope-like as Benny crouched like a cougar at the starting line garden hose while Coach Carlisle, from across the field, hollered: "mark . . . set . . ."

When the pistol sounded, I threw my gangly body into motion. Praying that I didn't reinforce my geekiness by slipping and falling in the damp grass, arms like windmill blades without the blade, I flailed through the November air. I didn't look for Benny. I expected he'd elbow me over at any moment and then step on the small of my back for good measure, so I just focused on the next garden hose, the one serving as the finish line. It appeared to be bouncing on the grass, one bounce for each of my pounding strides. I'm not sure if I looked more like a daddy longlegs spider or a jackhammer as I charged forward. I do think I felt a lung crack.

As I neared the finish hose, Coach C was yelling something and seemed very agitated or excited as I chugged closer. Crossing, I felt his hand pop me between the shoulder blades.

"Hey," Benny whined as he panted. He'd finished a step or two behind me. "I . . .. my . . . I tripped back at the . . ."

Coach C turned to Benny and looked him straight in the eye: "Not what I saw, Mr. Dentz."

Then he slapped me on the back again and grinned a broad grin. "I knew you could do it, kid."

~~~~

Johnny Carlisle's wife—or someone—had collected and painted some paper milk bottle tops of the day, fastening them to loops of fuzzy yarn lanyards to serve as awards. I received a gold one. Benjamin got a blue one.

I wore mine around my neck all that day at school and part of the next until the yarn busted and the thing fell off somewhere.

Crossing Paths with Edward Abbey 1966

TRUDGE. IT IS THE WORD THAT I DIDN'T GET RIGHT IN the fourth-grade spelling bee. What a stupid word, I thought, ranting to myself. Who'd ever use the word trudge? I'll never use the word trudge! (Curiously, in ninth grade, I would hold similar concerns about the entire concept of "algebra.")

In August of 1966, I found myself trudging up the trail that led from Juniper Lake to the top of Mount Harkness in Lassen National Park. We'd been camping at the lake for nearly a week, and this was the first day that it wasn't raining. Dad got us on the trail. "The view at the top will be spectacular," he said.

Mom had somehow forgotten her fancy Vasque hiking boots at home, so her feet were swaddled in Keds and socks with plastic Wonder Bread bags slipped over the socks to serve as waterproofing. She made it about a mile up the hill before she grumbled, "Enough!" and sat down on a rock in the sun. Brother Beebo, as I recall, stayed with her while Dad and I soldiered on.

The trail was rocky and muddy. Rainwater and snowmelt often filled the path. Frequently, after tiring of slipping and slogging through the muck, I'd try walking through the ankle-deep green grasses at the side of the trail where the footing was even worse. The leather boots I wore I'd about grown out of, and they weren't waterproof. I felt huge blisters forming on my cold, cold feet. But Dad prodded me onward. The meaning of that word from the fourth-grade spelling bee was becoming clearer and clearer with each step.

At a fork in the trail, I paused and looked at Dad. I remember peering down upon Juniper Lake and thinking, if not saying, "Okay, we've gotten to a nice view. Can't we turn back?"

Dad pulled a trail guide from his pocket and, as he pointed up the trail, he read: "The last section of the trail switchbacks up a cinder cone . . ." "Don't you want to hike on a cinder cone?" "No." Then, "Hikers can feel the grasshoppers dance at their feet . . ." "Don't you want to feel the grasshoppers dancing at your feet?" "No." Dad continued reading, "Once on top of the slope, the trail continues to the fire lookout. The fire lookout is staffed in the summer months and hikers are welcome to visit and learn about fire monitoring." "Don't you want to learn about fires and stuff from the ranger?"

That sounded interesting, and I was off.

As a kid, I was not a big fan of switchbacks. Wouldn't it be easier to simply climb straight up the hill? And on the north-facing glade on Mount Harkness, that's what I did, short-cutting two or three of them. The combination of the

Mt. Harkness Lookout (National Park Service image)

slope and the elevation squeezed the breath out of me pretty quickly. Panting, I waited for Dad to catch up, taking in the view of Lassen Peak to the west, a promontory called the Cinder Cone to the east and a number of lakes that dotted vast reaches of forests. A pair of gray birds that squawked like blue jays zoomed in and out of the scrubby trees that grew nearby. And there were flowers. It was like springtime in August.

The fire lookout atop Mount Harkness appeared like a great rustic lodge constructed of reddish-black boulders and rough-hewn timbers. The closer I got, the more magnificent it became. Only two stories in height, the thing seemed to loom over the mountain's top. The lower level was made of those boulders, quite possibly gathered from this very mountaintop. A steel door was centered on one face of this basement, and I don't recall if there were any windows. A wooden staircase climbed up one side leading to a catwalk that circled the outside of the structure. From the ground I could see that the entire top floor was framed in great windows, offering a view of, well, everything.

I stood at the base and looked up.

A slender man with a thin beard appeared through a door to the upper level. He looked at me, then glanced to see Dad several yards back.

"Okay if he comes up?" Dad must have nodded, because the next thing I heard was "Come on up, kid."

I climbed the stairs and circled the lookout on the catwalk. Mount Lassen was close enough to touch. Juniper Lake seemed directly below us and Lake Almanor, on the opposite side, almost as close. This may have been the first time I understood the concept of "seeing forever" that Robert Goulet sang about on the radio and Dad sang about in the bathtub.

The inside of the lookout was dominated by a table placed in the middle of the tiny space. Atop the table was a map with a weird looking sighting device that I learned was used to pinpoint the location of a "smoke." The interior was rustic and spare. Under the windows was a wire-spring bed, a tiny refrigerator, cooktop, and some primitive cabinets and shelves filled with canned goods and books. Mostly books, and a flute—which seemed out of place—just like the one Rebecca Langworthy played in beginning band back in seventh grade. All

"Was that you I saw shortcuttin' up the switchbacks?"

the woodwork was painted a pale green, about the same color as the Park Service trucks and Jeeps I might have seen earlier.

"Candy, kid?" The ranger dug into a drawer and pulled out a butterscotch round. "Is that your mama you left down on the trail down there?" He pointed.

"Uh huh." Not only could he see everything from up here, but he also noticed everything.

"Was that you I saw short cuttin' up the switchbacks?"

I gulped. *He noticed everything.* "Uh huh."

"Well, I'd like you not to do that on your way back down. It causes erosion because it wears out the vegetation that protects the mountainside. If the mountainside goes, so does my house here." He made a circle with his hand as he said this. "So please just trudge on down the trail like a good scout on your way back to camp, when the time comes. Understand?"

"Uh huh."

The ranger's hair was long and messy and his beard untrimmed. He wore heavy green trousers and a khaki shirt. He had a badge pinned to his chest, which meant he was the authority. A shine or a twinkle in his eye told me I wasn't in much trouble for having left the trail, but I knew I wouldn't do it again.

"You have any questions?"

My mind raced. *How do you get groceries? Ever see a fire? Ever see a bear? Do you stay here all year? Does it get cold up here? Does anyone ever come to visit? What do you do in your spare time? What do you do when you do see a fire?*

"When you have to pee, what do you do?"

The ranger laughed. Dad, by now, was standing in the door. I'm sure he was embarrassed. Come to think of it, I probably was too.

"Well, kid," the ranger said. I've got real limited facilities up this way. Down over to that stand of pines they built an outhouse. A privy. But I don't use that when I have to . . ." he looked at Dad. ". . . urinate. Out around this way," he pointed, "there's some rocks I use most of the time. Sun shines on it and evaporates most everything. Wind blows any stink away. And then, you want to know what's funny?"

I nodded.

"Around dusk the deer come up this way and lick the salt off the cinders . . ."

～～～

The late Edward Abbey was one of the West's great environmental voices of the latter half of the 20th century. His novel *The Monkey Wrench Gang* became a classic of the movement. Other works are clearly based on his experiences in various backcountry domains, including *Black Sun,* which centers on the despair of a solitary lookout stationed on the rim of the Grand Canyon.

Having read almost all his work, the last book of his that I picked up was a journal called *Confessions of a Barbarian*. On page 203, it reads: —

> *September 13, 1966—Mount Harkness: The deer—bony scrawny starving things, like giant mice, stare at me in motionless fascination when I play my flute for them—not amused or amazed, or puzzled or frightened, but simply . . . fascinated: silent wonder. They gather around the lookout and in the crater below in herds, as many as fifteen or sixteen at a time, counting fawns.*
>
> *Giant vermin, they'll nibble anything for a taste of salt—they even lick up my urine from the cinders . . .*

A Final Voyage *1967*

HUGE AND WHITE LIKE THE SPINDLY, PALE HAND OF a gigantic witch, the downed sycamore lay directly in our path. Beebo and I could see water piling up as the current tried to thread its way through the tree's carcass. Here we were: two idiot teens haplessly ill-equipped for navigating Dad's big wood-and-canvas Old Town canoe in such a swollen, raging stream. And clad in army surplus field jackets for warmth, not life jackets for buoyancy, damned easy to drown.

The mid-February paddle down Chico Creek from the Five-Mile to our home was supposed to be uneventful. And it was. It was until we ran under the fallen tree a few hundred yards upstream of the house. We should have known better—thought things through a bit more. Heavy rains had soaked the area the week before. The ancient tree toppled in a gust of wind one night. Mom swore she heard it go. Beebo and I went to investigate the very next morning.

The bow of the classic canoe slipped under its naked, angled branches. Wedged, the boat listed and twisted and pitched under the force of the creek's massive current. Icy water rushed in as slowly we tipped. We were going over. It was in this moment that the newsreel of my soon-to-end life flickered, and in that moment I caught images of the brief existence of our Great Old Town canoe. The one now pinned beneath the sycamore.

~~~~~

One of the most anticipated days of my childhood was the one in which a Delta Freight Lines cab and trailer backed the entire distance of the gravel driveway to deliver our long-awaited canoe. I stood watching as the teamster deftly maneuvered his huge, boxy trailer between our white rail fences touching not a twig on the rose bushes that clung thereto. Once positioned around a slight bend and in front of our garage and after the brakes on the semi exhausted a gasp of compressed air, the driver rolled open the van's rear door. Inside, a burlap-wrapped parcel, nearly the length of the entire trailer, lay on the floor. A tag fluttered from the near end. The driver grabbed the tag, pulled it free and asked, "One of you fellas named Clayton?"

Dad stepped up. "Give you a hand?"

~·~·~·~

The summer before, we'd visited Musty's mountain chalet a few hours away at Bucks Lake. Rimmed in pines and firs and rustic boat docks and cabins, Bucks Lake may have been the most enchanting place I'd ever seen with the possible exception of Disneyland. Musty's family's mountain chalet was glorious, all wood, set up the hill just a bit in a stand of trees that whispered through the night. An icy brook flowed across the property, and a small pool had been formed with rock and mortar in which beer, soda and watermelons were chilled. We could cook outside or in, and we could sleep outside or in.

A few yards away, a tiny, private beach proved perfect for wading, swimming and beaching boats. One boat was someone's turquoise blue wood-and-canvas canoe. Elegant lines, bent cedar ribs and ash thwarts, handwoven wicker seats, Dad was mesmerized. "A piece of art on the water," he said.

"It was built by a company called Old Town. Had it since before the war," someone named Uncle Wilbur said. "Wanna try it?"

"Holy cow! May I?" Dad asked.

"Most certainly." Uncle Wilbur handed Dad a paddle. "Just put the kids in life jackets."

Dad paddled us to the middle of the lake with a grin so broad he could barely clench his smoking pipe.

～～～

On his next day off, he packed us in the station wagon for a trip to Weeks and Emerson Boatworks, two hours away in Sacramento. This outfitter was the closest dealer of Old Town Canoes, and while there certainly were other canoe sellers around, and other canoes to be had, we weren't, according to Dad, going to get an aluminum boat that "looked like B-25," because "I spent too damned much time in one of those crates over Italy."

Once at that Sacramento dealer, Dad immediately asked about seeing a wood-and-canvas Old Town. A big one. A Guides Special. Something to carry the family and all our gear.

"Do you have one in stock?" he asked.

"Nope. We'll have to order one for you. It'll be three to four months," said Mr. Weeks.

"Three to four months?"

"Yep. They hand build 'em and only start one once it's been ordered. There may be a few ahead of you. Takes more than a few weeks to lay one up, then they got to ship it all the way from Maine."

"Maine?"

"Yep. The factory's in a village called Old Town in Maine. They've been building them there for over a hundred years. Still using the original forms and stretchers, I'm told. Lotta history comes with an Old Town Canoe," he said with a grin. "Lotta legacy."

I could almost feel Dad's pulse quicken. From a choice of only four colors, Dad chose forest green because it was, he said, "the color of the woods around Bucks Lake."

"It'll come slow-boat style on a freight truck, but I'll need payment in full to place the order," Mr. Weeks said, adding, "And you're gonna need a rack for that car."

～～～

Eventually, it arrived. My math today tells me our craft should have shown up in the middle of the school year, so I can't explain how I might have been home to witness the boat's arrival, but I clearly remember the race of my heart and the rumbling in my gut as that Delta tractor-trailer negotiated our driveway.

Dad unbound the boat from the burlap and placed it on a blanket on the garage floor. Deep green woods-around-Bucks-Lake color paint, graceful cedar ribs, light ash thwarts, mahogany trim: A big, beautiful work of art. Dad was ready to bust.

"It's a yacht," Mom said as she leaned her head to his shoulder. "It'll be our yacht."

I ran my hand across the woven wicker seats and readied myself to hop in as it sat on the garage floor.

"No!" Dad commanded. "Not 'til we put it in the water somewhere. Might scratch the thing up."

Then he stood there with Mom, swooning.

The Old Town Canoe

That summer and for many summers thereafter, our big, green Guide's Special would command attention at Bucks Lake, as well as Almanor, Black Butte, Shasta, Juniper and anywhere else we happened to put her in the water. Over the years of my growing up, we packed the thing to the gunwales, freighting supplies and camping gear, and vacationed for a week at a time in it. We also drifted down the Sacramento and Feather and lower Yuba rivers. We tipped it over and righted it just for practice. And we felt a pang of disappointment during dreary off-seasons when she hung in the dusty rafters of the garage waiting for spring.

In about '67 or '68, during a particularly wet winter, brother Beebo and I decided we'd like to take the canoe on a quick adventure down Chico Creek through the heart of town. Our property was fronted by the normally docile little stream, and the route would be simple. Put in at the Five-Mile Recreation Area, portage around the dam at One-Mile, drift through downtown and the Chico State campus, slip under the State Route 32 bridge and, a mile or more further, figure out how to angle the big green craft to the bank on our side of the creek and hop out.

An incredibly simple plan. But I'm not sure why Dad agreed to it. I'm fairly certain he didn't consult with Mom.

The Five-Mile Recreation Area was—and still is—a lovely swimming hole and picnic area maintained by the local parks district. In the summer, a lifeguard is present and a concession stand open. A diversion dam holds back just enough water for swimming. Families grill hot dogs and hamburgers, drink soda and lemonade, play Frisbee and softball. In summer, it is a mid-century, middle-America Rockwellian picture postcard of dappled sunlight, towering oaks, sizzling barbecues and frolicking children. During the wet season, the rec area is quiet, the concession closed and the lifeguard's chair empty. The diversion dam channels floodwaters into a man-made ditch called Sandy Gulch, directing any potential hazard away from town. This happened only on rare occasions.

And this winter would be one of those rare occasions. Four or five days of pretty steady rain had abated. The sun was out but the temperature cooler than it had been during the storms. Chico Creek was full, bank top to bank top, with a week's torrent of muddy water and snowmelt gushing out of the eastern foothills and rushing through town. The turbid excess pressed into Sandy Gulch.

Donning our heavy army fatigue jackets for warmth this February day, we put in just below the diversion dam. The water was running pretty good—fast and full—so we reasoned it should be a quick trip.

For the first half of the run, Chico Creek forms the main attraction for Lower Bidwell Park. We used our paddles not for propulsion—the current provided all the propulsion we needed—but to push ourselves away from the creek bank and muscle our way through eddies and swirls. From the paved roads that wind through the oak woodland on either side of the stream, we delighted in the whoops and exclamations of folks riding bicycles or strolling—folks who were wishing they were us. Most of the wooden barricade that served as One-Mile Dam was removed for winter, but a shallow, relatively still pool of water allowed us to slow, climb out, fumble the big canoe around the barrier and continue. We slipped under bridge after bridge through Chico's gridded streets and soon found ourselves gliding the stream course through the campus of Chico State College. More huzzahs and cheers, this time from students who likely would rather have been doing what we were doing than studying.

Just 25 or 30 minutes after we put in at Five-Mile, we were racing under the Southern Pacific tracks and the Highway 32 bridge. We'd probably make it home before Dad.

And we would have, except for that wicked sycamore.

~~~~

Around a blind bend, the rapid current pulled us toward the cavity left by the uprooted stump. Beebo tried to rudder us to the other side, and I back paddled like hell, *honest*, but there was no avenue to skirt the massive tree that reached all the way across the creek. Helplessly, we crashed into and under the great white limbs as the bow of Dad's classic canoe slipped into the tree's grasp. The force of the tumbling water pushed the stern sideways. We thrust our paddle tips trying to break free from the snag, but that action simply raised the downstream gunwales and tipped the upstream edge below the surface. We'd turned the boat into a catcher's mitt of current. As it listed, we slapped furiously at the creek's violent surface to pry ourselves back away. But the

Old Town was shipping water—now over the thwarts and wicker seats—the mass of which pushed us further into the sycamore's grip. Beebo hollered, but I don't know what he hollered. In moments, there came a rending groan and then a snap. One of the cedar ribs cracked. Then another. Then another. Unrelenting, the water poured into and over the canoe's carcass as we tumbled out. Down the raging creek we were carried, bobbing at first but soon weighted down by those damned army jackets.

In front of Musty's house, we came to a wider, slower section where a thick grapevine hung from an oak and skipped on the water's surface. Grabbing it, we pulled ourselves out of the water and slogged back to the scene of the now-derelict classic. The craft seemed intact. The stern pulsed and throbbed above the stream flow, but the bulk of the canoe was submerged, pressed to the creek bed by the furiously roiling water. Wading in to rescue the thing would be futile—we'd just be swept away again—and we knew we couldn't gain foothold on the muddy bank, grab the boat and pull it ashore. Drenched and cold-becoming-colder, we figured that the best course of action might be to wait until the storm flow passed and the creek subsided. We'd unwedge it later.

"Beebo muttered, 'Chico Creek didn't kill us, but I think someone's gonna.'"

Soaked and shivering, Beebo muttered as we slogged home, "Chico Creek didn't kill us, but I think someone's gonna."

When we arrived home, Dad stood at the foot of the driveway. Fists pressed into hips, he simply asked, "What happened?"

~~~~

Later that week, we salvaged the Old Town canoe. Save for one small tear, the canvas looked okay, but several ribs and one thwart needed the type of woodworking skill no one in the family possessed. Dad hooked in with an industrial arts student from Chico State who, for payment in advance, would repair the boat. Within days, he got started on it. Then he got drafted.

The remains of the grand old Guide's Special are now residing, as they have been for decades, in a semi-familiar place: the dusty rafters of somebody's garage. This time, brother Beebo's. Canvas stripped away in advance of replacement years ago, it is a project that will likely never see completion.

~~~~

In 2012, on a vacation to down east Maine, I sought out the original boat works in Old Town. The 1860s-era brick factory I'd seen in catalogs was long gone, replaced by a modern, sunny showroom. This 21st-century space smelled of chemicals and resin and was filled with fiberglass and composite and thermo-plastic paddle craft: river and sea kayaks, pedal boats and some canoes. All modern. All functional. All completely lacking grace, elegance, soul or craftsmanship. I wandered about, disappointed that the old building was gone and with it, apparently, the Old Town legacy.

Ready to leave, I passed the customer service counter just inside the front door and paused to acknowledge the young person manning the register. Then I noticed it. Behind that counter, pushed against a rustic-looking brick-and-barnwood façade, rested a stunning forest green canvas canoe. Slung just so, I could make out the woven wicker seats and the deeply shellacked cedar ribs, ash thwarts, mahogany gunwales and cedar planking.

My breath caught.

It was the spittin' image of the old Guide's Special, right down to the color: *the color of the woods around Bucks Lake.*

A sign standing in front of it read: "Not for sale."

Still, I inquired. "May I take a closer look?"

Incident at the Jolly Kone 1968

IN MY CAREER AS A PUBLIC-SCHOOL STUDENT, I WAS always walking distance from school. Rosedale Elementary was just across the creek. The junior high was across town, but town wasn't all that big. And the high school was through the orchards, across the Highway 32 and a few blocks down West Sacramento Avenue—maybe 25 minutes from home.

Located just through those orchards on this side of the highway, next to Aldredge's Bait Shop and Flying A, was a hamburger stand called the Jolly Kone. It was where I'd purchased the only pack of cigarettes I was ever to buy. I remember the place being erected when I was just seven or eight.

As a high schooler, while I was not involved in sports, I did engage in after-school activities, not the least of which was a Dixieland-style pep band I organized and conducted with a tuba wrapped over my shoulder. We'd scheduled practices twice a week, so rather than leaving campus at 3:15, it was likely 4:30 before I departed.

Fifteen minutes into the walk home, I'd near the Jolly Kone and begin to salivate over the wafting fragrance of frying beef patties and potatoes bubbling in some sort of boiling oil. For $1.35, I could enjoy a burger stacked with lettuce, pickles, tomato, some secret sauce—probably just Thousand Island—on a sesame seed bun before Ray Kroc popularized the notion. And the fries? Golden and crispy outside with steaming, almost creamy white insides, accented with just a touch of salt. The Coca-Cola came in a Styrofoam cup half-filled with shaved ice. Sitting at an interior table covered with oilcloth, I'd ponder Algebra II, the out-of-my-league redhead Rebecca Langworthy and whatever we'd just practiced in Dixieland. Finished with the burger and fries, I'd drink the remainder of the Coke and crunch on the ice as I walked home through the orchards, depositing the empty Styro cup in the garbage cans beside the tractor shed before entering the house.

Dinner would be almost ready, but I would only pick at it.

"You're a growing boy," Mom would say. "You have to eat your dinner," and she'd push a plate of chipped beef on toast—or whatever she'd prepared—closer to the edge of the table where I sat.

"Perhaps he's just going through a phase," Dad offered.

Mom insisted: "He's got to eat!"

I didn't.

～～～

Dad kept the weeds down or pulled the occasional stump with his old Ford tractor. Rather than store cans of gasoline in the tractor shed, he'd drive the thing through the orchards to Aldredge's Bait Shop so he could fill it up.

One afternoon after pep band practice, as I'm savoring my covert burger and fries, I hear a familiar voice order a strawberry milkshake from the outside window.

Dad!

Before I could determine that there was no escape, he appeared at the door to the dining area, sucking mightily on a straw filled with a thick, pink, viscous fluid.

"Son," he said.

"Dad," I responded.

He glanced at my burger, then at me and bit at his lower lip. No other words were exchanged.

Moments later he mounted the tractor and, holding the milkshake in one hand while steering with the other, disappeared into the orchards.

The remainder of the walk home took forever, but forever wasn't long enough. Dinner's aroma was filling the kitchen—something with liver—and was about to be served.

"Now you have to eat your dinner," Mom beseeched.

As I traced figure eights with my fork in the entrée, Dad looked at me from his end of the table. After a heart-pounding eternity, he said, "I think he's just going through a phase, Honey-Bee." He glanced up toward Mom. "I'm pretty sure he's not going to starve."

The First Grand Motorcycle Adventure *1970*

IT MIGHT HAVE BEEN A GOOD IDEA FOR ONE OF US TO carry a map.

The wilds of the Lassen National Forest are accessed by a maze of forest byways and logging roads. Although Stevie and I knew a couple of the roads as Humboldt or Humbug, in the forest they are referred to by a curious collection of letters and numbers: 20N24, 22E15 and the like. The intersection of Humbug Road and Jonesville Road was not labelled Humbug or Jonesville but rather two strings of letters and numbers. I figured the N and the E had something to do with north and east but was never sure about the digits that bracketed the letters. All we knew is that if at a junction we'd stay on a road with a particular number, eventually we'd end up someplace. Otherwise, why would they have put in a road?

Yes, a map would have proven handy.

Some of the great dirt roads of our world were in rugged, eastern Butte County, where the dry grassy foothills sweep upward into evergreen forests and the rocky cornices of the northern Sierra and southern Cascade. Accessing these roads on motorbikes with displacements the size of a seamstress's thimble was no mean feat.

"Neither of those bikes has enough poop to get out of their own way," Beebo snorted often when Stevie and I headed toward the hills.

And Beebo was right. Lots of miles of driving on shoulders of state highways, uphill, at full throttle, might yield 20, perhaps 25 miles-per-hour. Puttering up these grades we were often buffeted by the huge Diamond Match or Georgia Pacific Peterbilts, monstrous, howling log trucks racing from one of the mills in town, forestward, to grab another load of fresh timber.

Far up the hill and into the yellow pine belt, maybe 90 minutes from home, the paved road turns to dirt. A big brown sign welcomes passers-by to the Lassen National Forest. Stevie and I find ourselves still sharing the road with those big Peterbilts—now not moving so fast—and drivers of Jeeps, International Scouts, raised pick-up trucks and, where the road really got rugged, VW bugs. Exploring forest roads on a warming summer morning and into a pleasant afternoon proved as enjoyable as just about anything I could think of—especially since Rebecca Langworthy had just run off with Nilley.

My pal Steven Rios and I were just out of high school. Stevie's dad had let him have a motorcycle for some time. The Rios family had moved down from Cedarville, where they'd run a cattle ranch up on the Modoc Plateau. They moved because Stevie's mother wanted to "see people more than once in a while." Stevie's bike was a Honda Trail 55. Built in about 1964, it had a little sprocket and a big sprocket on the back so, when the going got tough, Stevie could add a half dozen or so lengths of drive chain, which gave the little tiddler a lower low gear and the necessary grunt to slog through mud holes and climb over stumps and boulders.

My mom was happy to simply let me ride a Schwinn until I was a high school graduate, and even then, the thought of her son on a motorized two-wheeler sent her into panic mode. "I'll not have you joining some gang!" She'd said this before. Perhaps the thought was shared by all moms except Stevie's.

It took some time to wear Mom down. But, with a $125 for a down payment and a loan from Laurentide Finance, a yellow Honda trail bike was mine. Stevie looked at my new yellow CT 90 and said, "Mean machine," then pointing to his smaller 55 said, "Sewing machine." But Stevie never uttered a word of envy. Country boys from up on the Modoc don't envy. They simply enjoy.

Onto the carrier of my Honda, we strapped a Safeway bag filled with the essentials: apples, beef jerky, a couple of cans of Coca-Cola. We reached the promised land of dirt roads

The First Grand Motorcycle Adventure   125

My Ticket to Freedom (American Honda Motors © 1969)

and deer trails by well before noon. By this hour, the summer sun had risen high and slipped through the forest canopy. The warm mountain air loosed intoxicating scents of fir and pine. Stopping to reconnoiter at a junction or just take in the view, the sound of the soughing pines or a burbling stream was enchanting. Mount Lassen seemed close enough to touch, and any road split from the one we were on simply became a road we had to explore.

On magic summer days, time meant nothing, and this was a magic summer day.

By mid-afternoon, out there somewhere, we came across a junction. The other road was labeled with the digit-digit-letter-digit-digit pattern followed by an X. We still had time to explore, so we opted for it. Slipping out of the forest of fir and pine, the road climbed over what appeared to be an old volcanic mudflow. Vegetation was sparse and scrubby, but tracks marked the route well. A mile or so on, we crested a rise and dropped ever so slightly into a basin. The road turned to softer dirt, and again we felt the freedom of effortlessly gliding through the forest. Making a huge clockwise arc, we noticed, through the stand of trees, a seasonal lake, now dry, which had filled the bottom of the basin. On we tiddled for, perhaps, two or three more miles, enjoying the scenery and the lowering sun. About 40 minutes from the junction, we came to a skidded-off area littered with slabs of pine bark. The road was now gone, but we putt-putted across the cleared area until we came to a cliff. It was at this point that we determined that "X" meant "Dead End," "No Outlet," or possibly *"Turn Back, Ya Idjit!"* Had we had a map . . .

Stevie and I were confronted with a sheer cliff and no road. The return would be about four and a half miles of Jeep trail that we'd already traveled. And in the deepening hours of a summer afternoon, the smooth, waterless lakebed begged us to cut across. We could easily save 20 minutes. We backtracked on the "X" road until we could thread our way through the woods and down to the playa. At the edge, Stevie broke out his extra chain lengths and took about five greasy minutes to install them. I flipped my bike into low range and simply waited. At this point, Stevie might have evidenced a glimmer of envy.

Firing up our bikes and goosing the throttles, we sped across the lakebed.

> **"Unless we took action, the bikes would sink to the bottom of the mire."**

Smooth as a highway and moist enough to not kick up dust to whichever of us happened to be second in line. Moist enough to have told us, had we been paying attention, that the dry lake wasn't exactly dry.

About 50 yards in, the crust broke. By about 63 yards, our little Hondas were mired to their foot pegs and axles. Their tiny engine putters were muffled by the sludge into which we were sinking. Stuck.

Killing the engines, we dismounted in mud so thick that the bikes both stood upright as if on their center stands. Shadows from the firs at the edge of the lake were creeping our way. We churned our legs to avoid from sinking in and initially laughed at the sucking noise made by the air as it rushed to fill the void between the mud and our feet. Then it dawned on us. Unless we took action, the bikes would sink to the bottom of the mire, and we didn't know how deep it was. And it would be about a 40-mile walk home.

Immediately, we grabbed the game rack on my 90. With what, to me, seemed like a herculean effort, we unsucked my Honda, pulled it back 20 or 30 feet and then, at Stevie's suggestion, laid it on its side. I imagined my beautiful ticket to freedom disappearing into the muck once again, but Stevie was a country boy from Modoc country, and I wasn't going to question him. Next, we slogged out to grab his 55. Tugging it free, we pushed it past mine, closer to the shore, then rescued the 90.

On solid ground, we straddled our two-wheeled mud puppies and set to firing them up using the kick starter. That was the point when Stevie realized the Converse All Star that had been on his right foot, one of the new pair his mother had purchased for him to wear at graduation, was no longer on his right foot. He looked at the once and future mudflat. Already our tire tracks and our footfalls were filling in with ooze. He shook his head and said, "Mom's gonna kill me" as he pumped down on the lever barefoot. One stroke and his 55 purred to life.

I was luckier than he. My big 90 cranked over with a similar one stroke, but I hadn't lost a shoe.

~~~

It was well after dark when we arrived back in town, having ridden the edge of the state highway with only the poor illumination of the trail bikes' headlights to keep us from slipping into a shoulder of gravel, busted glass and whatever had fallen off the last pickup load to the dump. I drove directly to my home as Stevie did to his. Parking my beloved, now broken in and mud encrusted, well out back of the tractor shed, I peeled off my muddy jeans, laid them over the bike's seat and attempted to sneak into the darkened house.

But in moments, the patio light blazed on. Blinded, I heard Mom demand: "And just where are your pants?"

I knew I had no reasonable explanation, but I was grateful that it wasn't me who'd lost a sneaker. I'm sure Mom would have asked. And that would have been tougher to explain than the pants.

Blessed Are the Meek *1972*

WHEN THE DRIED LEAVES SCUTTLE ACROSS AUTUMN'S harvested orchard floors, my mind shifts back to Gramma Carah. I remember rounding up those leaves with a worn bamboo rake, pulling them into a heap and trying to pick them up. She'd shown me many times, bending over the pile, one arthritic hand grasping the rake handle just above the tines, the other, fingers outspread. She'd scoop the leaves against her outstretched hand, pivot gingerly and dump the load into a rusty steel wheelbarrow with its wooden handles cracked along the lines of ancient grain. The conveyance had to be as old or older than she, maybe dating back to the gold rush. I didn't know. She rarely missed any leaf or twig she intended to have wind up in the wheelbarrow, and she always ended the procedure with a graceful sweep of the front of her threadbare plaid work dress. Then she'd say, "You try, David."

Mrs. Carah seemed about 100 years older than I, and maybe she was. It always amazed me that she could rake and

Rose Wild Carah as a young woman (Wm Carah Collection)

scoop leaves so well. Most every time I tried her method, a few would wind up in the wheelbarrow, but most would end up skittering across the dry garden and into a neighboring orchard.

"Try again," she'd say.

Eventually, when I'd get it right and most of an entire rakeful would land in the target, she'd say, "That's the system!"

I liked raking leaves with Gramma Carah. I liked the look of the fresh, tiny furrows left by the rake when we finished under a walnut or pecan tree. I liked pushing the wheelbarrow. She said she was too old to do it anymore. Even full to overflowing, it was light enough for me to maneuver out of the garden and across the gravel drive to a cleared area out back of the house. There, load after load would soon become a pile. She'd wad up a sheet of newspaper and stuff it just under the edge of the mass. Then she'd strike a match, saying, "You should always let an older person do this. Matches are not playthings."

Standing downwind, I'd let the smoke wash across my face until my eyes stung. I liked the mixed smells of the burning leaves and the last of summer's derelict fruit rotting under the apricot or peach tree. Somehow, I belonged here.

～～～

Rose Carah was not really anyone's grandmother; she'd never had the opportunity. Our neighborhood's cluster of kids knew her as Gramma Carah because that's how she referred to herself.

We used to traipse up the long, dusty road to her house on summer afternoons after a busy day of engineering a dam in the nearby creek and swimming in the pool we'd created until the current washed away our efforts. She'd always be ready for us. We were asked to leave our wet and, by now, muddy Keds on the front step. Once we were barefoot, she'd push the screen door open to the porch. Its spring-loaded hinge chirped a metallic, mechanical, musical sound and slammed itself shut after we charged in. She made us sit on the caned seats of wooden chairs. She'd moved them into the living room from the kitchen table, so we wouldn't put our wet bottoms on her good furniture.

Then she'd begin: "Which one of my little men learned a Bible verse for Gramma Carah today?"

We all fidgeted a bit.

"Now I know one of you must have learned a verse . . ."

"Blessed are the meek . . ." someone started.

"For they shall inherit . . ." she prompted.

None of us could remember.

"What will they inherit?" she asked.

"Peace?"

"Money?"

"Yeah! Money!"

"No, no, no, my little men . . ." She paused. "Blessed are the meek: for they shall inherit the earth."

We looked at each other, nodding in agreement.

Taking a faded volume from a shelf by the heater, she opened it and began to read, her rheumy gray-green eyes squinting from behind clouded wire-rimmed spectacles. The book was illustrated and full of stories. Stories about shepherds. Stories about angels. Stories about places we believed were far prettier than the little town in which we lived—the pictures proved this—and about people who were probably far better than we'd ever be. Afterward, we carried our chairs out to the kitchen where, along with a random and ever-changing selection of seashells, a pitcher of iced Kool-Aid was set about with Kraft cheese glasses waiting to be filled. Alongside was a plate of store-bought gingersnaps. As we crunched and sipped and toyed with the shells, she'd tell exotic stories about where they came from. Stories that lasted until we got fidgety.

Soon we were off, tramping back down the dusty road. She undoubtedly said to come back anytime. We had probably not said thank you.

~~~

As just another kid in the neighborhood, I visited with Gramma Carah often. She always had something to say about townspeople I knew or places she'd been. She told me about Mr. O'Biven, the fire chief after whom she'd named her fat, gray tabby; and Mr. Pullin, the elderly gent who still owned a bicycle shop where Mom and Dad picked out our Schwinns. "He was an old man when he worked for Andy Sr." she said. She talked about traveling through Yellowstone in a covered wagon. "I believe we were one of the very first groups through after they made it a national park," she said with pride. "Although I think Teddy Roosevelt may have been there just a week or two before us."

After the tale about Yellowstone, or the Mississippi or the Great Plains, she'd sigh and say, "My, my, but God's made a wonderful world for us."

She'd hug me, and I'd have to agree.

Sometimes she'd usher me into an otherwise unused room illuminated by a bare lightbulb with a pull chain. There would be her cache of seashells. She must have had millions of them. Each shell looked like every other, but each one held a geography lesson. "This shell came from awaaaay across the ocean, David, from a place called San Cristobal in the Solomon Islands. Do you know where that is?" I'd shake my head and she'd unfold a tattered map, saying, "Andy Junior sent it to me when he was stationed there with the air force." She pulled out a faded black-and-white of her son and, along with it, the gold star that I came to learn meant he wasn't around anymore. Then, with that sweeping motion she also used when gathering leaves, she'd say, "Andy sent me all of these."

Time would simply stop when she began to talk about her shells, and I found myself a helpless kid torn between feelings of tedium and fascination.

I remember our last visit. The autumn air hung heavy with the smoke from someone burning leaves in the area. Her house was to be razed in order to make room for a new apartment complex, so she was going to have to move. Progress, they called it. Older than anyone I then knew, Mrs. Carah certainly had to be too bone-weary to leave her home of so many years, so much time. The whole circumstance seemed ridiculous to me. Couldn't it all just wait?

Topping that, out of the blue, I was asked to deliver about a ream of documents and show her where to place her signature. "She remembers you. She likes you," her niece from down near Fresno said on a long-distance call.

Gramma liked everybody, I thought.

"How'd you get my name?"

"Oh, Auntie Rose talked about you and the Calvert boys a lot," the niece said. "I couldn't seem to get a hold of the Calvert boys. You up for the task?" Then she added: "Please? You'll save me a long day in the car . . ."

 I parked my VW at the foot of the narrow road that led the 100 or so yards to her house. As I walked up the drive, I tried to think of a way to keep this from happening. I could drop the papers in a puddle in one of the ruts, but it hadn't rained since April. Or I could lose them to a passing breeze, but the air was still. I could burn them in a pile of leaves. After all, I was old enough to use matches now. Or I could say I forgot them and just visit for a while. I kicked a pebble once, twice, and watched it dance up the road in front of me, then fall off to the side. Somehow that long gravel drive wasn't as long it once had been. I reached the front door with my gut fluttering, wishing I hadn't been so damned willing to save that niece from Fresno a long day in a car.

 Gramma Carah sat rocking on the screened porch as I mounted the step. I hesitated before knocking because she looked quite serene, and I wasn't sure she was awake. In that moment, I hoped she'd simply rise and start sharing some ancient gossip about Mr. Pullins or Chief O'Biven.

 "Mrs. Carah? Gramma?" I called just above a whisper.

 The rocking stopped. "I'm sorry," she apologized. "Do come in."

 I pulled open the ancient screen door, slipped past and waited for that familiar sound, positioning my foot so the thing wouldn't slam shut.

"My, my. You're getting so big and handsome." She lifted a hand from the arm of the chair.

"Please don't get up."

"Oh, well, I'm not sure that I could." A dry chuckle followed this. "Would you like to see some shells?"

"No, ma'am." I found myself lying again. "I just brought these papers over for you to look at and maybe sign."

She sighed and pulled an old, faded blanket that had slipped from her lap. "You know," she said, "I don't think I can see well enough to read them anymore. Do tell me what they say."

This was legal stuff. Outside of applying for a driver's license a year or two back, I don't think I'd ever done anything with anything legal.

"Oh," I stammered. "I think they just let those people know that you've agreed to sell the house and that you will have cleared . . . I mean moved out in about 60 days when the escrow closes." Then I added, "I'm not sure I know what 'escrow' means."

"Escrow. Escrow." She grew silent for a moment. "I've sold this house, haven't I?" There was another moment of silence. A longer one. "My but we had some fine times here, didn't we Andy?"

This caused me pause. "Yes ma'am," I said politely, wishing I had a hat or a baseball or something to turn in my hands—anything besides that sheaf of documents.

"Well, let me sign those papers," she said with an aged sigh. "Bring me my fountain pen from the kitchen table, won't you please?"

I ventured into the kitchen where no cookies or juice was laid out this day. I could not find her fountain pen. Returning, I said, "You know, Gramma, you don't have to sell this place to that realtor man. You could . . . You could . . . just stay here, you know. Me and the boys, we could . . ."

She raised a gentle hand, an understanding one, and said: "I can't stay here. I'm far too old. I can't cook. I can't see. I'd probably end up burning this old house down around me. Save them doing it once I'm gone." Her laugh was a bit more robust, adding, "Then what might you and the boys think about that?"

"Well," I said, slipping a Paper Mate pen from my shirt pocket. "I'd dispute whether you're ever going to be too old."

Another dry chuckle. "Please hand me the pen and something to write on."

I retrieved the well-worn children's book from the shelf near the heater and offered her the Paper Mate.

"Oh, I don't like these new-fangled ballpoint pens," she said. "Can't control 'em." Then she paused. "I guess there's fewer and fewer things one can control as we get on in life. Wouldn't you say, David?"

"I just turned 20," I said.

She looked up at me and a thin smile crept across her lips. Slowly she began scrawling her name—*Rose Wild Carah*—on dotted lines as I pointed them out to her. I leafed through page after page while she signed again and again.

When all was done, the process somehow completed, I said, "Some of the boys and me'll be over to help you when the time comes. It'll be a moving party. But you'll need to supply Kool-Aid and cookies."

"That'd be quite nice," she answered in a broken whisper. "But I'm sure I can do it all myself. I probably won't need any help." She fixed her gray-green eyes on mine and said, "Andy, do you remember a Bible verse for old Gramma Carah?"

A decade melted away. This may have been the first time in my life I'd actually felt my heart stop.

I thought for less than a moment. "Blessed are the meek: for they shall inherit the earth."

Head resting on the back of the chair, her eyes settled and closed. Soft sigh. There she sat quietly, gently rocking and that thin smile returned.

I waited for a moment.

"Blessed are the meek," I whispered and, careful of the old screen door, quietly slipped away.

Roommate *1975*

IT TURNED OUT TO BE A LOUSY RIDE DOWN THE OREGON coast. Perhaps it was the wind and fog. Wind and fog are no fun on a fancy BMW motorcycle like mine. Then again, perhaps it was the traffic. Or maybe it was because, in contrast to US 395, a desolate, high desert highway 300 miles to the east, US 101's coastal route seemed like a carnival midway. T-shirts. Ball caps. Souvenirs. Rides and attractions. Signs that read: "Congestion."

But I knew it was none of those things. I knew it was the news I received when I phoned home from Astoria at the mouth of the Columbia.

I was sure of it.

～

In college, my enrollment in symphonic band found me connecting with an upperclassman named Richard—don't-ever-call-me-Ricky—Fiero. He played trombone. The first day of rehearsals something immediately sparked in him—

something for Christa Harper, the best friend of Jenny Leone, the young woman I would eventually, if only temporarily, marry. I remember Christa as innocence personified, walking into the band room that first day of rehearsal, clutching a narrow, worn out Artley flute case, looking as confused as a kitten in a windstorm. She was clad in a prim, pleated skirt and a soft, curving cashmere sweater, and at least two dozen eyes focused on this Christa, including mine. Richard pointed to her and said to all the others in the lower brass section, "That one is mine," and by Richard Fiero's pronouncement, designs any of us may have had were immediately quashed.

Richard served as an older brother while mine was off in the army, and being band guys, I roomed with him for a while. He convinced me that a man needed a smooth and soft lambskin leather jacket, a face needed a daily dose of Aqua Velva and that a Trail 90 with a seven-horsepower pot-metal motor and no clutch was no real man's real motorcycle. No. His customized Honda 450 was what a college man needed to drive. So it wasn't long before I had a motorcycle of larger displacement with upswept pipes, two cylinders and a clutch.

Together, Richard and I commuted from our rented 10 × 50 Nashua mobile home north of town, down to campus for band and a couple of other classes, usually on our bikes. Richard always rode in front. Sometimes, if it was foggy or if it might rain, we'd cruise to class in his beloved, custom-painted Chevy El Camino with polished Cragar mags. Never would he be seen in my Volkswagen.

One drizzly evening while we were heading back from a night class, some kid tossed a rock at the El Camino and put a prominent ding just over the rear wheel well. Richard screeched to a stop right in the middle of Bryant Avenue. He threw open the door, reached under the seat and retrieved a .22 that I didn't know he had. "I'm just gonna scare that little son of a bitch." For I don't know how long, I sat, wide-eyed, in the darken middle of Bryant Avenue as the Chevy's exhaust wafted in through the open driver's door.

Eventually, Richard returned uttering only, "Shit."

~~~~

Besides band, one of those other classes was Anthro 101. Richard and I weren't pretending to be smart. We were lower brass players. Big. Dumb. The interior linemen of the university band, learning with distinct disinterest about the aboriginal cultures of the Lesser Antilles. The motive for enrolling in Anthropology was anything but academic.

Christa had chosen to be an Anthro major.

It wasn't long before Christa and Richard married, then Jenny Leone and me. Richard served as my best man. He coached me on how to adjust the cummerbund—a stupid accessory if ever there was one—how to stand just so, even how to look longingly, committedly into the eyes of my bride. Christa was Jenny's maid of honor, doing in silk and gossamer whatever maids of honor do.

Within the course of a few semesters, the four of us completed college and earned teaching credentials. We rented homes and eventually became buyers. We got real jobs: I as a classroom teacher, Richard as a high school band director. In short, we became all that a 1970s society expected of young people graduating college. A few years later, Richard's career prompted a move to Sacramento, two hours south, then, as their version of the American Dream became further elusive, to Texas, where Richard gave up band directing and began a commission-based gig hawking Herff-Jones product—class rings, letterman's jackets, chocolate bars and the like—to schools for fundraisers.

Meanwhile, as our eighth anniversary rolled around, Jenny and I fulfilled another 1970s expectation and filed for divorce. By that time, we had a house and a daughter but little else. Certainly not each other.

I'd call down to Texas to see what was going on with Richard from time to time, but he was always somehow otherwise occupied. Maid-of-Honor Christa spoke only one sentence to me clearly ever again: "I don't know why he would want to speak with you anyway."

Distance, I supposed, creates distance.

Or, maybe, divorcing one's best friend.

～～～

Arcing along one of those windswept viewing turns below Seaside, I am thinking about how integral the motorcycle has been in the 30 years since I last saw the fellow who introduced me to one. The salt-laden fog is something to be experienced, and it can't be done inside a car or motor home. Nor can the still, settled smoke of evening campfires when riding through a forest after dusk. Nor the moisture in a river hollow. Nor the exhilaration of a sweeping turn that crests a ridge affording a view of the next 10 miles of enchantment. The BMW I am riding is a machine better than I deserve and perfectly suited for the rises and twists of US 101 up this way.

So as I'm riding south, I'm thinking of Richard and how much I assume he'd enjoy roaring along in front of me on his customized 450. How much he'd light into me if I were to enter a curve too fast and venture into the oncoming lane.

"Damn it, Roomie," he'd curse. "Focus! Don't get distracted! Look through the turn or you'll get all catty-wom-pus and crash into something. You'll lose your goddamn teeth! Break your skull! Shit! Even die!"

He would've expressed things similar had he known about the incident that happened before he and Christa moved out of town. A distressed phone call: something about an overflowing sink and Richard was away at rehearsal. Me rushing to the rescue like some latter-day knight on a white stallion. Potato peels, it turned out to be. Potato peels stuck in the J-trap. Climbing out from under the kitchen sink. Wiping my hands on my trousers. Christa had slipped away after pointing to the sopping towels and puddled floor. Now she was wrapped—no, draped—in a soft white robe sashed ever so loosely at the waist and smelling of fancy soaps or bath salts or something lavender.

I stood in Richard and Christa's kitchen. Facing Christa. Staring at her. Wide-eyed. My buddy Richard Fiero's Christa.

Me. Stupid. Twenty-two or -three. Two years married. Too-young married. Not knowing how to react or what to do. Frightened. Frightened to death. Fight or flight or something like that. Christa's intoxicating aroma . . . presence . . . still lingers, haunting me about this singular, delicious, forbidden . . . I've wondered about it over and over. She . . . It won't let me go.

~~~~

And that's what I was doing—wondering—at this moment while rocketing down the coastal highway. *What . . . what if?*

Approaching a cliffside bend way too fast, I struggled to punch a downshift and leaned deeply into the curve. Not deeply enough. The guardrail came near. Too near. My booted ankle brushed its metal surface and a low hanging branch slashed at the upper arm of my textile jacket. Overcorrecting, I swerved into and across the oncoming lane and onto the opposite shoulder just as a loaded log truck whistled by, air horn blaring. A fall was going to hurt like hell. Trying to maintain balance on the rocky surface, I squeezed the brake, and slowly, I came to a rest, upright, on the gravel apron.

Inside my helmet, Richard's voice boomed: "Damn it, Roomie."

Followed by Christa: "I don't know why he would want to speak with you anyway."

Legs straddling the big Beemer, feet firmly planted on the ground, I didn't dismount but stood over the bike and loosened the helmet. Composing myself. Taking inventory of my heartbeat and my heart, thinking, *There's something I need to learn from this moment*; then, *No. There's something I need to learn to forget.* I probably stood that way, facing oncoming traffic, for 15 minutes, until a pleasant OHP officer stopped to check on my well-being.

~~~

That news from the night before: I had called Mom from Astoria, as I did from time to time when on the road. "Just checkin' in," I said and informed her of my whereabouts.

Mom cut me short: "I heard something real disturbing down from San Antonio last Thursday . . ." Mom said. "I don't know exactly what happened. Jenny did something with that computer of hers and was able to pick up a story from the San Antonio paper."

"What'd it say?"

"You'd have to ask her."

Then I called Jenny.

~~~

My old roommate liked cans of Nally's chili because it was an easy dinner to fix. He liked bottles of RC Cola with those peel off *look-underneath-and-win!* cap liners because sometimes he found he'd won a quarter. He liked steak, Olympia beer and female pop singers like Dolly Parton and that coal miner's daughter, although he made me swear I'd never tell anyone in the symphonic band. He liked being one of 76 trombones and didn't want anything to mess that up. He liked hot rodding in his El Camino with his lambskin jacket on and smelling like a rich man. Richard liked a lot of things.

But he loved Christa.

Periodically, when I called to chat with my growing-up daughter, Jenny would let me know what was going on with Richard and Christa, and I hoped she passed along my greetings whenever she spoke with her friend.

Christa, it turns out, developed something called Chronic Fatigue, and with it, MS, a crushing combination that makes it first psychologically, then physically impossible to hold a job. As the damned thing advances, it becomes more and more difficult to shop and do those chores that make life, life. Eventually, there's no getting out of the house. And for some, no getting out of bed.

Honoring and cherishing, for Richard, became clothing and bathing, feeding and comforting and focusing solely on his mate. Her needs. Their love.

As things progressed, Jenny often told me, the bond shared by Richard and Christa just seemed to grow. Followed by, "They sorta caught the fairy tale we couldn't quite grasp, don'cha think?"

I was never quite sure what I thought.

~~~~

I stopped at a lookout point somewhere around Gold Beach to stretch and to see if the surly crashing of the ocean might provide insight into, or, at least, respite from the news of my day. My mind first drifted to Christa: her whisper, her fragrance. And those regrets I wasn't quite sure how to own. Then to Richard. I was indignant that he would choose this time to ruin my long-anticipated north-to-south journey along the fabled Oregon Coast. Cliffs. Coastline. Harbor Seals. Darting carefree from cypress tunnels into sunlit prairies and pausing for a cup of chowder at Mo's—all were things I'd hoped to savor this day. But the rhythms of the ocean and the road were absent. I might as well have taken Interstate 5.

I sat on a concrete parking bumper next to the bike, ran my fingers through my damp, helmet-pressed hair and squinted into a salty western sun glaring off the late-afternoon surface of the Pacific.

"Cancer," Jenny had said last night. "Cancer. Richard found he had inoperable cancer. Something on his brain." Then she hedged, "At least that's what everybody's saying."

～～～

So here's the best I could figure: Richard loved Christa more than anyone should love anything other than maybe God. As her condition advanced, the beauty of Christa in springtime became clouded with pain and angst and who-knows-what. To be sure, that change—that sad and inglorious change—became evident to everyone except the fellow in whom a spark ignited some 30 years before in the band room at Chico State.

For Richard's whole life, caring for Christa was his highest calling. Loving Christa.

Thus when Richard knew time would take him from her—rather than the other way around; when he knew there would be no one to care for her in his singular loving, perfect manner—he engaged in love's final act.

I assume he said a prayer.

I know he told her he loved her.

And I suspect he also said, "I'll be there for you. Always."

The San Antonio paper reported that they were discovered by a worried son, the .22 still clutched in Richard's hand.

~~~

At Jedediah Smith Redwoods State Park, back in California, after a daylong ride down the scenic Oregon coast, I told the ranger that I only needed to stop and use the restroom. At my age, every 50 to 70 miles one has to do this. "Just need to stop for a minute," I said as I fumbled for my wallet from which to extract the day-use fee.

"Nah," the seasonal said with a grin, waving off my contribution. "Go on ahead. The restrooms are the first left past the Interpretive Center."

At a picnic table, in the dusk-muted shade of centuries-old Sequoias, I sat for a moment, smelling the settling smoke from 50 evening campfires and hearing the gleeful cries of children frolicking through the darkening woods. I thought of the complexities of my day's travel south on US 101. All those what-ifs from decades back. What if I'd never been talked into a real motorcycle? What if I'd truly been committed to Jenny, looking longingly, lovingly the way I'd been coached by Richard? On the other hand, what if, after those wet towels and potato peels, I hadn't unconvincingly muttered, "No. This just . . . this . . . this isn't right," and then, in a burst of anxiety or confusion, barked, "I fixed your damned drain now I gotta go!"?

And what if Richard knew . . .
What *did* Richard know . . .
I shook my head to see if I could chase away those thoughts.
No luck.
After a spell, I pulled out a postcard and, in the gathering darkness, scratched the following:

> *Dear Roommate,*
> *Damn you one helluva lot for screwing up my ride home down the Oregon Coast! Shit, man! But, at the same time, thanks for giving me the opportunity to enjoy so many roads. Man-oh-man! The places I've been on one of these things, thanks to you.*
> *You were a prince.*
> *I have missed you all these years, and I shall continue to miss you, brother.*
> *Christa was a lucky, lucky woman.*
> *I am sorry for all the pain . . .*
> —Roomie

Even though there was nobody to send my note to, halfway between the Smith Redwoods and where I was to stay in Crescent City that evening, I found myself consumed by the need to find a postage stamp. If not tonight, then tomorrow.

Leon *1977*

"YOU KNOW, KID," THE OLD FIRE BOSS SAID, "WE DON'T put these forest fires out. They go out."

I'd sat down next to him at the so-called captain's table, a teetery assemblage of planking and sawhorses set atop uneven dirt and duff and rock near the fire camp's commissary. This table was reserved for VIPs such as myself and for the captains and crew chiefs that directed operations against the massive Skinners Mill wildfire of 1976 or '77.

Why was I a VIP? I delivered the groceries.

～～～

Back then, I earned a thousand bucks a month during my first couple of years as a teacher. Good money, I thought when I'd been hired, but not enough, it turns out, to support a new wife, rent, payments on a '74 Volkswagen bus and, well, food. So I took a summer job as a teamster pedaling freight for a small, regional company called Peters Truck Lines. The Teamsters, I soon found out, proved more effective for their members than did the California Teachers Association. In 10 weeks of summer trucking, I made nearly as much as I'd made in 10 months of teaching. Plus, by pushing a pallet jack and lifting and loading boxes eight to ten hours a day, within a week or two, I found I was in the best physical shape of my life. Ever.

Peters Truck Lines low-bid a contract with the US Forest Service to deliver perishables to fire camps throughout Northern California. One day, the boss called the Chico dock from his headquarters in Yreka, and shortly after the phone rang, the foreman came out to the loading dock, pointed at me and said, "Kid. Get the phone. God wants to talk to you."

Walt Peters, the company owner, would be on the other end of the line. The company's main office was up north in Yreka because Peters thought Yreka was God's country. I'd been informed of this earlier, along with, "Unfortunately, nobody ever told Walt he ain't God."

I took the phone. "Fire camp runs. Willows up I-5 to Corning then west into the Coast Range past where the pavement ends out there somewhere."

Sounded like an adventure.

"All the hours you could want. Could last a week or more. Straight time, though. No overtime pay."

I did some mental math. Straight time for eight plus time and a half for the next four, versus . . .

"Well?" Walt barked.

"I'll take it."

"Take the GMC reefer and a fuel card. The cooking crew'll be a bunch of inmates—prisoner trustees, some of 'em felons—doing the last year of their stretch. They get two days knocked off their sentence for every day they work the line. Be careful what you say to 'em, got it?"

He paused for that to sink in. "Now, go home and pack a sleeping bag and a toothbrush and a change of duds," he said. "And don't forget to kiss your wife."

God had spoken.

~~~~

The run from Willows to Corning and up into the hills took a good two hours—maybe a little more. In Willows a crew stuffed my 22-foot refrigerated bobtail with caseloads of beef steak, pork chops, bacon and halved chicken. Waxed cardboard cartons of lettuce and carrots and all manner of vegetables were stacked in, as were crates of dairy including milk, OJ and eggs. The GMC was happy enough running up the freeway loaded, and my mind wandered to the only experience I'd ever had with wilderness fire when I was about twelve . . .

Dad and I crested a small ridge and began the descent into Summit Lake, where we'd parked the car by a ranger station. I wandered off the trail believing I smelled something weird, like a spent campfire. By a naked sugar pine about 50 feet from the trail. A tiny thread of smoke wisped from the forest floor. I felt the ground and it was hot. Dad joined me.

"Damnation of Faust," he muttered. "We'd better let someone know."

I lit out for the ranger's outpost.

Panting, out of breath from exertion and elevation, I poked my head through the open portion of the Dutch door.

"Whatcha need, kid?"

I pointed back up the trail. "Smoke. Comin' out of the ground..."

In the 15 or 20 seconds it took for the ranger to sling on his pack and grab a Pulaski that was propped in the corner, he said: "Lightning. Three days back. Damn thing will trace down a tree and lay there for a week or more, down in the roots, until... poof. The whole forest goes." And he sprinted up the trail.

The fire I was now working—the Skinners Mill fire—I'd been told, had been sparked by lightning and the whole forest was going.

~~~~

The fire camp was located 15 miles up a Mendocino National Forest Road roughly graded for area logging. On my first run, I tiptoed the GMC over the rocks and washboard. The commissary was situated on a small rise just beyond where the little road split into two rugged dirt tracks, and each led to ends of the kitchen area. Having been told at the dock to take the right fork first, I nosed the rig up the hill. Immediately, a huge denim-clad kitchen crew inmate started hollering and frantically waving his arms.

"Gawd damn, man! You got to back that truck up here. We got to unload off the tail. No turnaround at the top."

Hoping not to expose my woeful lack of experience as a truck driver—but much to the entertainment of the dozen or so work-release fellows on the cooking crew—I backed down to the junction and engaged in countless y-turns until I could trundle the rig up to the target.

"You get done on this side, you drive down to the fork and back up the other side. Got it?"

After less than an hour of hands-on learning, including jolting over a monstrous rock or root on that other side, and having been admonished: "That truck don't belong to you, so you don't need to baby it. You gotta make better time," I was on the road to Corning and Willows loaded only with empty crates and pallets to be refilled back at the dock.

I made the round trip three and a half times in my first 24 hours. My sleeping bag would never be unrolled.

~~~~

One trip, a day or two later, found me arriving at camp well past dusk. By this time, I knew the reefer was loaded with groceries destined for the right fork—meat and produce—positioned toward the tail, and items slated for the left fork—dairy and such—stacked toward the nose.

The only time I was supposed to enter the chill box was after the inmates finished off-loading. My job was to downstack the crates of milk and eggs, spreading the boxes and crates across the floor so that they wouldn't teeter and topple over as I rumbled up the other fork in reverse.

Climbing into the box that particular evening, I was greeted by the big inmate. He seemed to always be there. I was beginning to think he was in charge of something. Or maybe he was just big.

"You ever sleep?" I asked.

"Nope," he said eyeballing my skinny frame. "You ever eat?"

It being a month into my summer driving gig, I was feeling fit at six-foot-four and about 156 pounds. "You're the one that told me I need to make better time," I said. "Now I gotta break down this freight so it won't fall over while I'm getting over to the other side."

He set his feet on the floor of the truck and pressed his massive hands against the stacks of crates. "How's about I just stand back here and hold it all in place?"

I didn't know what to make of his broad grin. He towered over me, outweighed me by perhaps a half a ton and had a wingspan that could seemingly touch both walls of the reefer box interior.

And he was a felon.

The idea didn't seem like a good one, but I chose not to argue. I climbed into the cab and inched the rig down toward the split.

Backing up the other rutted dirt track should have been easy. I'd done it a few times by now. But it was nighttime and some genius at the top of the hill decided I could see better if he positioned a Jeep up there pointed down the hill and turned the headlights on to illuminate my route. The glare of the high beams rendered my mirrors useless. I twisted them away. I'd be backing up blind using braille navigation—memorization of the bumps in the road—to boost the truck to its destination.

At the bottom, I shifted into compound low reverse, stood on the gas pedal and jolted up the hill. About halfway up, I hit that damned root-rock bump—the one I should have remembered—at a pretty good clip. The rear duels jounced over the impediment, and the whole truck lurched violently. My head snapped back, hitting the back of the cab. I struggled to keep the throttle floored. Over the whining roar of the GMC's engine, the grinding spin of the four rear wheels and the spitting of gravel and duff, I could hear the collapsing of crates of milk and eggs as they hit the bed of the reefer box, along with the big inmate's muffled, "Gawd damn!"

Along with a lump on my head, something like a rock formed in the pit of my stomach.

Completing the scramble to the top, I bolted from the cab wanting to punch the idiot who'd blinded me with the Jeep's headlights, which now illuminated the carnage in the back of my truck.

The rock in my stomach became a boulder.

"Gawd damn!" the big man bawled again, covered in eggshells and yolk and trying to gain some traction in the slurry of milk and eggs and OJ that had gushed onto the floor. "Gawd damn!" He slithered off the truck's tail, landed on his feet and slapped me on the back. "Come with me!"

With a big hand clamped to my shoulder, the denim-clad man ushered me out of the floodlit loading area. I didn't know the lay of this land even in the daylight. I only knew where to drive to and where to drive out and that I was encouraged to make better time. A short newsreel of my 24-year life spun in my head as he propelled me through the darkness. And I remembered that I had not fully obeyed God's command: I'd not offered my wife a farewell kiss.

~~~~

Looping out from the storage area behind the kitchen, his grip loosened as I was marched to the front of the line where weary firefighters were queued up for chow. Still partially coated in egg batter, he elbowed me in saying, "You boys step aside. This here's the most important man in camp. He be the man who brought you all this food to eat."

Scattered applause rippled down the line.

A heavy paper plate was suddenly thrust into my hands with a steak about the size of Idaho laying across it. A denim-clad mess worker plopped a baked potato on top.

The big man pointed. "Over there. Go on. Over there."

An empty folding chair sat next to the old fire boss who motioned me to sit next to him at the captain's table. The boss then hollered to the inmate: "Leon, you get over here too. We've always got room."

Leon sidled in next to me and set his plate down. He leveled his eyes on mine and with his broad grin said, "Gawd damn! I do believe that's the best excitement I've ever had since I signed on with this outfit."

With that, he shook his head and slapped me on the back again.

"Now eat."

My Run-in with Elmer 1977

ACCORDING TO HIS COURT TESTIMONY, ELMER E. SHANNON left King Kue Billiards about 3:30 in the afternoon after having dropped not one but two nearly full bottles of Coors on the floor. The barkeep suggested Elmer was about through for the day. Elmer reported he'd said, "That's okay," because there was somewhere else he had to be. Then, he clambered into his early '50s-era Chevrolet one ton and headed across town to a doctor's appointment. Moseying south on Mangrove Avenue, Elmer must have missed the fact that the light for him at Vallombrosa had turned red.

That's when we met. I was heading home from my shift delivering freight for Peters Truck Lines. Astride my tiny Honda 90, I entered the intersection confident that oncoming traffic was slowing to a stop. About 20 feet in, like a gnat hitting a battleship, I collided with the side of Mr. Shannon's old pickup. He'd moseyed right through the red light. The bike and I went down mid-intersection.

Unaware, Elmer continued for a few hundred feet until somebody who'd witnessed things somehow got him to pull over. Meanwhile, I rose to my shaky feet in the middle of the intersection, taking inventory not only of my physical condition but of the condition of my up-until-that-moment preferred means of transport. Outside of the raggedly torn fabric on my best pair of Levi's 501s—damn it!—I was uninjured. Righting the Honda, I found that the front fork was shoved backward and the wheel wouldn't rotate, so I probably couldn't push it out of the way.

The light changed. Immediately, someone laid on his horn, urging me to move out of the way because I was holding him up. I gave the driver an I'll-be-just-a-second wave, but Mr. In-A-Big-Hurry pounded on the horn once more. I was about to offer the motorist the universal single digit of disdain, when a couple of college boys stepped in and hoisted the bike onto a traffic island, leaning it up against the light standard.

Leaving it there, I hobbled over to a nearby phone booth, where I dropped in a dime and waited for brother Beebo to rescue the bike and me.

～～～

Months later, on what would be the first day Anne Houghton served as a Municipal Court judge, I found myself subpoenaed to tell what happened. Prosecution questioned me. Defense counsel was an attorney named Spats Jones. As it happened, in those days my mother typed legal depositions and court transcripts for Spats at three bucks an hour. When it was his turn, Mr. Jones asked only two questions of me that I could remember: "What were you wearing?" followed by "Were those dungarees?"

I wanted to reply *Who the hell would care, Spats?* but didn't.

Elmer took the stand, stated his name, address and age, which was 68 and, on direct examination from the prosecutor, said that he'd dropped a couple of beers "over 'ta' the King Kue" and then headed out because he had a doctor appointment across town.

Judge Houghton interrupted.

8   Judge Houghton: "Mr. Shannon. You'd been drinking?"
9   Elmer: "Yes, ma'am."
10   Judge Houghton: "Before your doctor's appointment . . ."
11   Elmer: "Yes, ma'am."
12   Judge Houghton: "Then you got in your truck and drove
13   to the doctor?"
14   Elmer: "Yes, ma'am."
15   Judge Houghton: "How many beers had you had?"
16   Elmer: "I know I dropped two of 'em."
17   Judge Houghton: "Meaning you drank them, or they fell
18   to the floor?"
19   Elmer: "Fell to the floor, ma'am."

The Defense, at this point, was screwed. Spats Jones knew it.

20   Spats Jones: "Elmer . . . Mr. Shannon, what did you find
21   out at the doctor's office?"
22   Elmer: "I missed the appointment. They made me come
23   back another day."

24 Spats Jones: "Well, what did you ultimately find out? What
25 did the doctor say was the matter?"
26 Elmer: "Doc said something about a tunnel. Said I couldn't
27 grip things because of a tunnel. I didn't see no tunnel.
28 Hell, I didn't even see him."

He pointed at me and grinned sheepishly. Reflexively, I lowered my gaze. On the witness stand, Elmer looked like such a lost, broken old man. *Perhaps, by my entering the intersection, I'd placed him in this position?*

29 Spats Jones: "Did the doctor say something like, perhaps,
30 carpal tunnel?"
1   Elmer: (pauses) "Yeah. That might be it. Where is that
2   one?"

I saw Spats Jones nod at Judge Houghton. He then turned and winked at me. I didn't know why. My gut told me that Spats Jones and I had ganged up on Elmer E. Shannon, and I didn't like the feeling.

3   Judge Houghton: "Mr. Shannon, I'm going to ask you to
4   hand me your driver's license and I'll have the bailiff
5   arrange a ride home for you."

Shortly after court adjourned and after Spats Jones told me, "Say 'Hey' to your mom for me," I walked down a dimly lit corridor and saw Elmer sitting alone on a bench outside the bailiff's office door. Waiting. Waiting, I suppose, for that ride.

I felt a sad urge to say something to him—to tell him everything was going to be all right—something like what Dad might have said to me if I'd had a bad day or was confused about something. It'd been an accident, a simple wrong-place-wrong-time accident. I'd lost a good pair of Levi's dungarees, but I hadn't been hurt, and now he was probably never going to be able to drive again.

But I couldn't muster the words, so I kept walking down the hall.

I had the little Honda repaired and then traded it for something bigger and fancier.

About four years later, my mother called to say that Elmer E. Shannon had "made the obituaries," the not-so-quaint phrase she used when she'd seen in the newspaper that anybody anyone might have ever known had died.

~~~~

A couple of years back, I was retrieving a cold can of Coca-Cola out of the fridge when it dropped on the floor and spewed its goodness all over the kitchen. This wasn't the first thing that had slipped from my rather numb grip recently: a butterknife, a house key, a pair of pliers, a partially depleted bottle of Glenmorangie 12. The totality of these inci-

> "I felt a sad urge to say something to him . . . something like what Dad might have said if I'd had a bad day."

dents prompted a call to my general practitioner. A referral to a physical medicine specialist followed, which led to an uncomfortable and a bit intrusive electro-muscular/nerve assessment.

A few days later, the verdict was delivered: Probable carpal tunnel.

The leaves of my mental calendar fanned like the thumbed pages of long-forgotten text and the breeze they created chilled me deeply.

I was then 68.

Just like Elmer.

October Visitor   1983

IT WAS THE SECOND OCTOBER I'D SPENT IN HER HOUSE, a house that, until quite recently, belonged to a Nellie E. Petty. I'd purchased it from her estate, moving in with an old Amana refrigerator, an old chest of drawers, a piano salvaged from the Baptist Church and Anapest, the Siamese cat.

Divorce is a lonely thing. Being a bachelor had seemed far better than being married when I was married. But, as it turned out, being alone wasn't better than much of anything. Summer days were passable, but as winter descended even the hottest of roaring fireplace fires fell short of keeping me warm. This night, sitting near the glowing fire, I began the arduous task of reading some student essays. Over the song of the hissing and crackling fire, a cold wind buffeted and shook the old house. Autumn's dry leaves scratched across the window glass like wicked fingernails of someone or something itching to get in. Unable or unwilling to concentrate, I rose, stoked the fire, poured myself a second glass of Zinfandel—I'd just discovered Zinfandel—and watched the embers rise and fall. Anapest leapt up and corkscrewed herself into my lap, sighing cat sighs. My student's essays would wait. I stroked the Siamese's blue-point ears and sighed myself. Her broken purr perfectly matched my broken existence.

~~~

The house had been built in 1922: a California bungalow with a low roof line and a heavy stucco exterior. Kitchen, service porch, formal dining, two bedrooms, indoor bath with both hot and cold water and toilet, wood framed double hung windows and canning cellar down below. A covered, concrete porch faced Eighth Street, suitable for an evening sherry accompanied by a quality five-cent Roi-Tan cigar or an inviting chat with neighbors or passers-by. Quite the thing in the 1920s. World War I was a fading memory, and prosperous Happy Days Were Here Again.

Then there was that fireplace.

The realtor told me that Mr. and Mrs. Petty were the original owners. The house was the first of four properties she'd scheduled me to see, and I said there was no reason for me to look any further. I paid the asking price.

~~~

You see things once you've moved in that you didn't notice when you were house hunting. Weary, threadbare carpet was going to need to be replaced, as was the linoleum in the kitchen. And the whole place could use paint—inside and out. And the dining area: the dining area was a square room with no windows smack in the middle of the house. From that space you could access the living room to the front, all the other rooms to the side and rear, but, originally, not the kitchen. Someone, Mrs. Petty, I suspect, deemed this a bit impractical, so she encouraged someone else, Mr. Petty, I suspect, to cut a large, arched opening in the wall between the kitchen and this middle room. Mr. Petty did a fine job forming a near-perfect curve in the top of the passage, so access was much more efficient from stovetop to table.

Trouble was, with this hole in the wall, my refrigerator, the big old freezer-on-the-bottom monstrosity, had to be placed on the slightly sloping floor of the screened-in service porch. Tough to get eggs or milk or butter from the back porch through the screened door to the stove or counter for food preparation. I suppose there was a compromise involved. Or maybe the Pettys simply had a smaller icebox in the '20s and '30s, one they kept out back next to a wringer Maytag or Whirlpool.

Within months, I realized that the arrangement was not one I cared to live with. So, one summer's afternoon, I drove to the local lumber yard and picked up some two-by-fours, some lath—not easy to procure in the modern days of gypsum board—some plaster, primer and paint and set about closing this entry to the middle room.

"It will be good to have wall space," I said to myself and to Anapest, the Siamese, who wrapped herself around my ankles as I measured heights and widths.

Construction was relatively easy. Studs. Lath. Chicken wire. Plaster. Tools were simple too. Hammer. Circular saw. Trowel.

I wasn't too handy with the trowel as it turned out, and while I could scrape up the plaster I'd slopped onto the linoleum on the kitchen side of the project, the best remedy for the middle room was to simply remove the fouled carpet, exposing a gorgeous oak floor that I hadn't known was there. I finished the interior room's new wall with recovered wainscotting from a tear-down a few blocks away, topping it with 50% off grass cloth from a design store that was going under.

Many an evening, in subsequent months, I would stand in the middle of the middle room, stroking Anapest's blue-point ears and marveling at the prowess of my home improvement skills. The kitchen now accommodated a spot for the big Amana. It partially covered where the arched passage had been. Now, as with every well-planned efficiency kitchen, a triangle existed, apexes of which were the stove to the left of the old opening, the refrigerator to the right and the sink across the room. There was even a place to tuck a new Rubber Maid trash container between the stove and the wall. Easy to access, but out of sight.

～～～

The 1920s had been a decade of American fortune and promise, but I was existing in the 1970s, when half of those couples who got married ended up getting divorced. Living with just a cat, the refrigerator was always pretty close to empty. A half-gallon of milk would go bad before I could finish it, but I wouldn't buy a quart because, what if I should run out? Bread would grow moldy in a cupboard as I could never use up a full loaf before it expired. Popcorn, however, wouldn't go bad, and neither would beer. And oatmeal was a fail-safe for breakfast so long as I insulated it from the weevils.

Berne's Market, a long-standing mom-and-pop grocery, was a block west on Eighth Street. On special nights, I'd visit their meat counter and grab a pork steak. Coupled with a bag of spinach for a salad, for me, this was livin' high. Dining in that dark middle room, I often wondered if Nellie E. Petty felt the same way I did during the 25 or so years she occupied this bungalow after her husband had passed on. I pictured her driving an old Hudson six blocks to town or to the beauty parlor for color and curl, strolling over to the park a few blocks north, walking over to Berne's once the macular degeneration set in, and then finally confined to this lonely house—*for how long?*—after getting out was no longer safe or possible.

I suspect she knew this old place as well as she knew her own soul.

Deep in the winter a few winters back, I was told (realtors are required to disclose such things) someone—a church lady or a relative—coming to check on Nellie found her.

At peace, I suppose.

~~~

> **Cats sense things before people do.**

Cats sense things before people do. So, in retrospect, I know Ana knew. I know because just as I was drifting off and, probably only moments after the cat had relaxed into a slumber, she tensed.

A sharp gust of wind slapped leaves against the window, rattled the screen door to the porch and something went bump in the kitchen. In a twinkling, Anapest sprang off my lap. I clambered out of the chair to follow her.

Flipping on the light switch, I made a quick scan of the kitchen. Knocked over between the stove and the wall patch, the Rubber Maid lay on its side. Ana would have charged at some pork fat, but on this October night, the hair raised on her shoulders and over her arched spine. She backed away and, finding my ankles, curled nervous figure-eights around them.

I stood over the tipped trash container in silence.

Pondering. Wondering.

Finally, I whispered, "Mrs. Petty? Nellie?" Perhaps this was actually that red wine talking.

No response.

I waited a moment.

"Nellie," I said again.

Then, reaching down to pick up Anapest, I backed away toward the living room. If Mrs. Petty was somehow in the kitchen, I sure as hell didn't want to corner her. Moments later, the screen door to the service porch rattled and slammed.

A draft of cold air blew in and slapped me across the face. Anapest bolted from my arms and disappeared.

Waiting, pondering a bit more, I gingerly stepped forward and righted the plastic trash can.

Then it dawned on me: the archway—the work of her long departed—was gone. Sealed. Closed forever. Nellie had tried to pass through it but couldn't. Confused, disoriented, lost, she accidentally upset my trash as she attempted to find her way out of the kitchen. Her kitchen.

That must be what happened.

It has to be.

"Mrs. Petty," I said just above a whisper, probably to no one. "I'm takin' care of your place. I really am."

There would be no response.

Because it wasn't Nellie's place any longer. My comment was met with only complete, cold October silence—silence except for those leaves scratching across a windowpane somewhere else in the house.

A Road Trip with Dad *1992*

THE FIRST JACKSON HOLE WRITERS CONFERENCE would be an opportunity for a road trip with Dad. It had been years since we'd father-and-sonned it. So, not knowing what to expect from a writer's conference and willing to offer Mom a week's respite, I crammed Dad next to me into the diminutive cab of his '83 Toyota Hi-Lux, the one he could no longer drive. In the pickup's cargo box were tossed my suitcase and Dad's duffel. Stuffed behind the seat was a large bag of beef jerky I'd dried, a half-dozen Granny Smith apples, and Dad's favorite chocolate chip cookies: a traveler's lunch.

As we departed, Mom said, "Now you're going to find out just what it's like."

The look I returned must have been quizzical as I thought, *Find out just what* what *is like?*

Ready to roll out, Dad laughed and said, "Did you pack some beer, son?"

"Naw. It'd just get warm ridin' around in the back. I'm pretty sure we can find places that will sell us beer on the way, Dad."

Dad in his element

"You're sure?"

"Uh-huh. Pretty sure."

Thus outfitted, we took to the road.

~~~~~

Dad grew up a desert rat. Bent toward curiosity and never one to stand still for very long, he was always one to wonder about by what lay just beyond the horizon or over that far away ridge. *What must be on the other side?* he'd ask his

> **There is romance in discovery, in tired feet, in whistled tunes on the trail, in campfires and in the West.**

boys. By profession a letter carrier who slung a postal sack over his shoulder and walked the neighborhoods of his route, vacations always involved a backpack and a remote trail in California's Sierra Nevada or Cascade Range. Sometimes I'd tag along, listening to him whistle and watching him rhythmically swing the walking stick he'd fashioned from a rose cane. There is romance in discovery, in tired feet, in whistled tunes on the trail, in campfires and in the West, Dad wanted me to know. And although his mind was transitioning from gray matter to dust, the suggestion of a road trip to Wyoming rekindled a sparkle in his once sapphire blue eyes.

Two dawn-to-dusk drives across Nevada, southern Oregon and Idaho landed us in Jackson, Wyoming, then less a tourist destination than a way station on the road to the Tetons or Yellowstone. The kitchenette room we rented was in a low-roofed mom-and-pop cinderblock motel, a remnant of the early motor age, I suspect. A block or two from the Snow King Ski Resort where that first conference was held, our lodging was also just two or three tree-lined blocks from Jackson's small and intimate downtown. This would be a fine home base from which Dad could engage in a little wanderlust while I attended sessions.

"Leave a note," I asked as I trooped off to class, and it turned out Dad would do so, signing it "Clay."

~~~~~

I'd driven through the upper Snake River region a few years prior. Perhaps that's what attracted me to the first Jackson Hole Writers Conference. The scenery is stunning. If the conference turned out to be a bust, at least it would be a bust in a beautiful place.

During the welcome address, I recall the coordinator, a Jackson area resident, saying, "Writing is a lonely task. And I found I had no one to talk to about my writing . . ." So he organized an opportunity for writers to come together to discuss their craft, encourage one another, and, perhaps, free some new voices. He wanted to create a community. That first year's attendees included bestselling novelists, folks with screen credits, writers of historical fiction, poets and memoirists elbow to elbow with agents and publishing house editors; all elbow to elbow with neophyte writers and wannabes like me. Craft sessions taught things I hadn't figured out. Keynote speakers shared the rugged paths from pen-and-paper to publication. Panel discussions, one in particular, highlighted the tension between the folks who create and those folks necessary to ensure one's creation sees print. Visits in hallways introduced one to another, each somewhere on the dreamy road to bestsellerdom. Participants could have a piece read and reviewed by several someones already successful in the industry, and I did, nodding knowledgeably about comments made that I didn't fully understand. One reviewer picked up on my innocence or ignorance and, later in the day, over a beer, took me aside and said, "Let's go over this again."

Community.

Grilling pork chops after opening a bottle of red wine I'd picked up at the King Super, I gushed to Dad about what I'd learned, who I'd met and what I knew I needed to do next. Tomorrow and Saturday would be more of the same. While cooking, I chattered like an athlete pumped up because he tossed a game-winning touchdown pass or hit a shot at the buzzer. Inspired, encouraged, excited: whatever was running through my head that evening, I spouted to Dad.

Over those chops I finally asked, "How was your day?"

"I walked around some blocks."

The sparkle was gone from his eyes, and he didn't say any more.

~~~~

Day Two involved more sessions, more readings, more conversations with the very successful, all capped off with a stroll in the woods followed by some wine and some cheese. A presenter—a poet—asked me, "Where have you been published?"

"So far," I said, "I've just shared with friends and family. In fact, I brought my father along, out from California." It was the only thought given to Dad that day.

"Oh," she said with downcast eyes. Then she suggested that letting friends or loved ones read your work might not be the best editorial decision because they are obligated to love you, and love often gets in the way of honest criticism. I'd received eager opinions from my circle of friends, probably useless. Was their encouragement a roadblock to my own success?

I returned to the motel around 6:30 muttering about this, only to find a note: "10:15. Off to town. Clay."

But no Dad. Laying my participant portfolio on the dinette, I set out for a little walk about town. Surely, our paths would cross.

Jackson's frontier character had not been lost by the 1990s. Worn boardwalks fronted businesses on a bingo card grid of streets. The free space was a town square set about with antlers, towering trees, public art and benches. Perhaps Dad had settled onto one of these. Fellow participants milled about the square, chatting, connecting, networking. I just looked for Dad.

Thinking he'd been heading to our motel by a different street than I'd taken to the square, I returned to our room. Empty. Circling back toward town, I retraced some steps, then broadened my route to blocks farther from the town center. Darkness crept about, and I revisited the square, wanting to scrutinize everyone sitting on a bench in the gathering shadows without actually looking at anyone. Across the street, honky-tonk music thumped and clattered from an Old West saloon. Jaywalking in the semidarkness, I headed for the source of the music, thinking perhaps Dad, although not a country music lover, might have slipped in for a beer. He was a beer lover, after all.

"Five bucks," a big man said.

"What?"

"Five bucks. Cover charge."

"Hey, I'm just looking for my dad. An old man. Probably . . ."

"Five bucks."

~~~~~

Dementia steals its victim's mental capacity one or two brain cells at a time. Like a candle, once tall and erect, the individual melts and shrinks and flickers until, ultimately, the flame dies. Alzheimer's is not diagnosed with certainly until a postmortem is performed. This creeping form of dementia is attributed to many factors, all guesses: alcohol use, cooking on aluminum cookware, tobacco, chemical exposure. Dad, himself, in lucid moments, would say losing one's mind is a direct result of having raised two boys through their teenaged years. Then he'd laugh at his own joke.

I believe the first signs involve a stroke or mini-stroke with oxygen being denied the brain for a brief but critical period. Shortly after I'd married, I walked over to my folks' nearby house to swipe a cookie or borrow a hand tool. Perhaps I could share a Lucky Lager or two with Dad after he got off work. As it turned out, Dad had wearily pedaled home from the post office that day. I found him collapsed on what used to be my bed. Raising his head from a slight slumber, he turned and mumbled a greeting. The right side of his face was both stiff and slack, and I couldn't clearly make out what he said. One sapphire eye shone while the other looked blank. With effort he flexed his jaw and slurred, "I don't know what's wrong, son."

I ran home and collapsed on my own bed in tears and fright.

A decade later, we'd be on this road trip to Jackson.

~~~~~

I pulled a $5 out of my wallet and ventured in. Darker than the dusk outside, it took a few moments for my eyes to adjust. Rows of whiskey bottles were placed on shelves backed by a large plate mirror, seemingly doubling the inventory of hooch. Being Friday night, every stool at the bar was taken as were all of the tables and shadowy booths. Across the venue, on a well-lit stage, an overweight front man, clad in too-tight Wranglers, a snap-buttoned shirt unsnapped a bit too far, a white Resistol hat that likely had never seen a dust devil or a cutting pony, belted out something country while squeezing dissonance out of a lime-green electric guitar. Backup band members offered a throbbing beat that vibrated my bones. Any intimate conversations between couples would have to be shouted over the din. Dad wouldn't be in here—he preferred Broadway tunes—but still I probed the corners and scanned the shadows, past the dudes and their partners drinking whiskey and wine. There appeared to be no real cowboys here. Nor Dad.

I didn't bother to ask for my five bucks back.

Night had fully enveloped the square, and as my anger for this disruption bubbled, I felt my way back to the empty motel room. The Westclox on the wall read 9:10. Shit!

The house phone was a push-button desk model. After pressing "9," I called the local police.

Within six minutes a tan Teton County Sheriff's Dodge pulled up. The deputy opened a back door, and Dad unfolded himself from the caged back seat. As I stood, hands on hips, he spread his arms and cried, "Son!" There was excitement in his eyes and his face beamed.

The deputy approached before I could unload. "You know this man?"

"He's my dad."

"Susan at dispatch says he came through the door around 4:00. Says he said he wasn't lost but he didn't know where he was. She hung around way after her shift, says she was worried about him."

The anger bubbling in my gut was replaced by something cold. It might have been guilt.

The cop stepped closer. "Is he, you know, okay?"

"Yes. No." I didn't want to say the word in front of Dad. "Yes. And thank you."

"Well, not a problem. I'm just glad it all worked out."

But it didn't, I thought. Instead of getting my money's worth outta this conference, I'm gonna have to babysit . . .

~~~~

Forty-five minutes north of Jackson on US 89 rise the towering peaks of Wyoming's Grand Tetons. I recall being struck by the rustic, weathering barns set in the lush meadows dotted with bison and elk, the peaceful nature and rugged sublimity of it all.

I remembered Jenny Lake backed by an infinite azure sky with those marvelous peaks mirrored in her waters and tender willows and stunted pines ringing the pool. It is a natural thing for me to eye such vistas, wonder where paths might lead and picture myself, pack strapped to my back, ascending with growing anticipation to a yet undefined but undoubtedly spectacular view from atop the craggy summit. *What must be on the other side?* It's my old man in me, I suppose.

Jenny Lake would be our destination, Dad's and mine, on the last day of the first Jackson Hole Writers Conference. We hadn't eaten much of the beef jerky on the trip to Wyoming, and four of the six Granny Smiths remained. On the way out of town, I stopped at the King Super and picked up a 12 pack of NA nonalcoholic beer. Dad dug through his wallet, somehow remembering that he carried a Golden Eagle pass affording us free entry into the park at Moose Station.

Heading north, as the park's grandeur unfolded, I pointed to a cluster of buffalo grazing in a Snake River meadow. "Bison, Dad."

"Cows?" Dad asked, turning to view them as I slowed.

"No, Dad. Buffalo."

"There aren't any buffalo anymore, are there?"

"Right there." I pointed.

"Cows."

The Teton Park Road offers a slower and more scenic alternative to US 89. Expansive views of the Snake's valley and the buttes beyond to the east would be considered spectacular were they not inevitably compared to the jagged, iconic glaciated saw-toothed range to the west. Sometimes hidden behind a curtain of pines, sometimes bare and naked and reaching toward heaven, the Grand Tetons stirred something in my belly. Glancing at my passenger, I caught a similar stirring in Dad's blue eyes.

"Where are we?"

"The Tetons, Dad. The Grand Tetons. Wyoming."

"This is real George. Real George. You suppose we could go for a hike?"

"Sure."

Turning left toward Jenny Lake Lodge, I threaded the Toyota down a narrow one-way strip of pavement. A widened viewpoint offered the vista across the lake I'd hoped for. Out of the way for others, I backed the tiny pickup into position. I figured we could drop the tailgate and just sit for a spell. Maybe have a beer.

"Let's have a look."

Dad sat in the front seat. "We're facing the wrong way."

"Let's just get out and have a look."

Jenny Lake and the alps beyond were framed between two gnarled pines. I could make out trails scratched in and out of sparsely treed side canyons and over naked, rocky lateral ridges. I wanted so to be on one with Dad. Nearer our little Toyota, willows tangled the shoreline. Verdant meadow grasses flourished as if springtime planned never to go away. A deeply worn fisherman's trail wound through the grasses and traced the edge of the lake.

Dad pointed at the path. "That's real George, son. You suppose we could hike it?"

Lake water gently lapped the shore. A soft breeze set the pines into gentle chorus. With Dad in the lead, I found myself again traipsing a high-country trail in the Sierra, California's Cascade or the remote reaches of the Coast Range. Through glades of mule's ear and stands of fir, Dad whistled, as he always did, and swung his rose cane walking stick. An eleven-year-old me tagged along behind, struggling to keep up.

Shortly, Dad stopped and, making sweeping arcs with his empty hands, said, "Well, I suppose it's getting late. I guess we should turn around."

It was not yet midday. I glanced over my shoulder. The parking area was still within sight. "Yeah. I guess so."

Fetching the jerky, apples and beer, I sat down on the lowered tailgate and patted its metal surface. Cracking open a couple of NAs, I said, "Sit." I looked toward Dad, who'd made his way to the passenger side of his pickup and was rummaging through the glove box. In a moment, he sat down next to me and after slapping his Chromonica three times on his palm, ventured into a flawless version of "The Sugar Blues."

The glass surface of Jenny Lake rippled under an errant breeze and the reflection of the Tetons dissolved. And as he finished playing, the mountains reappeared.

I don't know how long the pause lasted before he said, "This is real George, son. Real George. You suppose we could go for a hike?"

~~~~

The summer sun sets late in the latitudes of Wyoming. A purple dusk gathered, with a chilling breeze racing across water's surface that set those pines to whispering again.

Golden swaths of alpenglow illuminated the mountaintops. Jerky gone, beer too, and apple cores left in the grasses for the deer or the elk, we'd made a day of it: 71-year-old father and 39-year-old preteen son, sitting on the tailgate, hiking and sitting some more. Not talking much, however. Dad couldn't seem to find words.

But he did play his song. More than once.

~~~~~

Among the things nobody ever told me was, don't bring a distraction to a writers conference. While a well-orchestrated writers conference builds community, it really is a business meeting. The business of a writers conference is creating an inspiration that will ultimately manifest itself in print. Business meetings require the full attention of those who attend. I know this because in my professional life, as a public-school administrator, I'd run countless meetings that required the full attention of those attending. *You must be present* and *present*, I'd admonish my staff at the beginning of each new academic year.

Any inspiration I received at the first Jackson Hole Writers Conference dissolved on the long drive home, not because I allowed it, but just because it happened that way.

~~~~~

The candle that was Dad flickered out two or three years after his last road trip. I'd long harbored regret for missing the final day of that first conference years ago. I'd regretted missing the talks, the workshops and the community. I'd regretted my opportunity lost.

As time has advanced, regret I once harbored has faded like the ripples on a high country lake. The reflection has cleared. Now, when I think of the day, I close my eyes and I'm sitting on the tailgate of a little Toyota pickup, looking across Jenny Lake at the Grand Tetons, watching Dad as he climbs a scree slope up the distant, opposite ridge. He is swinging his cane walking stick, and I hear a whistled tune drift over the water.

Ultimately, he makes it to the crest and disappears through the crags, and as he does so, I wonder what he is about to find on the other side.

Gathering Sticks for a Fire *1998*

PART I

THE FOREST GLEN. ZIBE SIMPSON DETESTED IT. HOME would always be some place they'd lived before. Either the high reaches of the coastal ranges west of Orland, California, or the little farmstead near Chico, with its fruit orchard and flower garden. It would never be the Forest Glen, with meals as bland as spackling paste; where residents cup their hands to their ears while visiting about teeth, joints, how the kids never drop by; and where big screen electronics blare continually in the common areas to keep the dying awake a few days longer.

"People shouldn't live like this," Zibe said.

Or so Eleanor reported.

They'd postponed their move until this two-room flat came available. From the second-floor unit, the old couple saw forestlands to the north and a promontory called Sawmill Peak to the east. The views recalled the free, high country and times far different from their current circumstance. Once sheep herding in the Coast Range and fruit farming in the valley: now living in the fading fabric of personal history.

Zibe found refuge in a little woodshop out behind the complex. It didn't matter if he had a project. The Glen's ratio of seven women for every man meant this hideaway was nearly always empty. He dabbled with an assortment of hand tools that would otherwise remain unused. Completed works, thick with a yellowy, pungent finish, rarely made it to the tiny apartment on the second floor. "Too much clutter already," Eleanor would remind him. "Remember, we decided to cut back when we moved here."

He made occasional trips to the local Builders Supply, taking care in selecting his purchases: a handful of brass screws, some white glue, half pint of varnish or paint. Perhaps a quarter sheet of plywood or some short lengths of two-by-six. His sundries had to fit inside a 1988 Ford Tempo. Always a Ford man, this compact and largely plastic Tempo fell well short of the trustworthy old F-250, his truck of a generation ago.

Ultimately, life led to this: a largely plastic automobile and the Forest Glen Senior Residences. Here, with the pines and the mountain out the window and with access to a little communal workshop, Zibe tied a tiny knot in the end of a final thread and hung on.

Or so Eleanor reported.

~~~~~

"My father and me and my brother, we used to run sheep all over this high country ever' summer. So did his dad, my

Aiton." Sitting by the campfire, he drank Carlo Rossi *vino da tavola* from a tin Sierra cup and chewed on a Dutch Masters President.

I watched the flames subside, with tiny, glowing structures dissolving and collapsing into ash. Subtle layers of darkness encroached. Across the fire ring, Zibe's glass eye—not the red, rheumy one he called "the good eye"—his glass *replacement* eye, reflected the glowing embers. He remembered his family's yesterdays.

Basques living on the west side of the Sacramento Valley, he told us, "Would run sheep up the Grindstone and graze 'em in the high country south of the Yolla Bollys. The trip up'd take the better part of a week."

Cattle folks ranged in the section as well, but while cows could forage throughout the yellow-pine belt, the sheep men tended to stake out the high, placid glades and meadows where the grass was tender well into early autumn. Once the sheep nibbled a section down to dust, the herder would usher his flock through a stand of forest to the next meadow.

"Back to when I was a kid, we herded 'em with Model T Fords," Zibe said. "Gravity feed from the gas tank under the seat to the carburetor. Got to going up a hill too steep and the damn thing'd starve itself and cut out. *Shee*-it! Found myself bouncin' down some hill lookin' over my shoulder more'n once. Jumped outta one time, 'fore it crashed into a tree. Fixed it by poundin' out the fenders with a single jack."

He laughed and sucked on his cigar; it glowed through the campfire smoke against the gathering night.

"Finally, *Aiton* said he'd take that damned hammer to my head if I ever skidded his Tin Lizzie down the glade agin. So I learned me to push them sheep up the grade by drivin' that ol' Ford in reverse. You know. Backwards. Like this." He made jittery arcs with a hand extended to an imaginary steering wheel, twisting his head to look back over this right shoulder. "Gas'd work that way."

I couldn't stifle a laugh.

"What? You don't believe me, little man?" I felt his eye bore through me.

I shook my head and headed off to my bedroll.

That night I dreamt about herding sheep through the high country and backing an old Ford up the hill. I woke the next morning with a crick in my neck.

~~~~

In the late 1960s, about 70 crow-fly miles distant from that camp at the crest of the Coast Range, the Simpsons resided on a little farm plot. It rested across Chico Creek from our five acres. By then, Zibe's sheep herding days were over. He and Ellie and their son Eric grew peaches and pears and corn and zucchini, sharing the produce up and down their block and with us.

I was never sure how Dad and Zibe connected. It might have involved the two of them clearing the channel of the creek prior to a rainy season, and I suspect it involved a couple of Lucky Lagers after the day's work. The result was that they became hiking buddies as well as beer buddies. Dad's schedule as a letter carrier afforded him a Friday-Saturday-Sunday weekend once every six weeks. And once every six weeks, the two of them would head for the "high grass country," as Zibe referred to it. Once, I tagged along on an overnighter with a pack frame slung over my back. Lashed to it were my sleeping bag and a red, two-pound box of Premium Saltines.

"That's quite a load for a little man," Zibe said when I first hefted the thing, making me flush with pride. Then he added, "Wish my boy Eric would do this. He don't know what he's missin'."

The Simpsons were lifelong residents of the region, and there was much for Zibe to show off to newcomers such as us. On fall and spring weekends, he and Dad would depart for the foothills east of town, "Yahi country," Zibe called it, and in the summer, they'd head off to the higher reaches on the other side of the Sacramento Valley, "My old stompin' grounds," he said. "Like the high Sierra only better because so few folks know how to get there."

On joint family visits to Zibe's high country outpost, I would play fetch in the meadow with Jovanna, their Boxer, explore the forests pretending I was an Indian, dam up the tiny willow spring creating a pool to wade in, and make myself useful, as Zibe would suggest I should, by gathering sticks for the fire.

After dinner and after a few swallows of red wine, he would light up a Dutch Masters and begin to reminisce about the romance of his youth, spinning yarns about days tending flock and night sleeping under dark, crystalline night skies

Mom and Ellie cooking at Simpson Camp

with "stars so close in you could touch 'em." Sweet, tantalizing cigar smoke mixed with smoke from the campfire permeated the clothes I wore—the same ones I'd wear tomorrow and forever until we returned to the valley and home.

"One time I sensed a big cat at the edge of the clearing, just kinda paddin' along. Out that way." Zibe pointed, then circled his hand over his head. "It was darker 'n this that night. Couldn't hear him, couldn't smell him. But I knew he was there. There was just somethin' about how the flock had laid themselves in that night." He paused.

A downslope breeze slipped across the fire ring. Flames danced wickedly, then subsided. I edged closer to the dwindling light.

"I don't know, maybe it was just an old coyote," he said. "I know we was down one the next morning."

There were stories every evening: stories of lamb birthings and of black bears rumbling through; of long, sunny days watching over the flock and gay Saturday night hooplas over at Smith Camp.

"Sometime back," Zibe recalled, "this slick-haired gov'ment dandy, packing a fancy leather attaché and wearing polished shoes with waxed laces—waxed shoelaces!—had big ideas about where we could and couldn't run sheep. Come drivin' up here in a big ol' round fendered Nash." He spat into the coals. "Somethin' about a de*lee*terious effect on the natural balance. *Shee*-it! The bastard kicked us and the Smiths and the Seguras and ever'body else off." Then he added, "A Nash. On that road?" He pointed through the darkness toward the route we'd come down.

~~~~~

By the time Zibe introduced us to his old stompin' grounds, Forest Service signs and a few telltale ruts were all that remained to suggest anything ever happened amongst the ridges and swales of the coastal range. Most place names offered history only vague hints of the folks who grazed livestock for a few months' respite from the summer heat on the west side of the valley.

But Zibe wouldn't let the record die.

Son Eric didn't understand the mission—or maybe he was just doing what sons of a certain age do. One evening at camp, as he was cleaning dinner dishes, Eric carped, "Dad, I'm gonna miss the Indianapolis 500 again. Jim Clark's running his Lotus and . . ."

"I don't give a damn about your Jim Clark," Zibe said, looking him squarely in the eye, noses nearly touching. "We need to do this. It is our history. It is who we are." Then he paused. His voice softened, and he'd corrected himself. "Who we *were*."

Eric crawled into his bedroll as the rest of us sat around the campfire. He summoned Jovanna, who had spent most of the day lazing in a bed of Mule's Ear foliage, to cozy up at his feet. As we absorbed his father's history, Eric read a copy of *Sports Car Graphic* until his plastic flashlight failed.

Morning dawned with Eric scouring the glove box of the F-250 for fresh batteries. Meanwhile, the rest of us breakfasted on bacon and eggs, Tang and biscuits that Ellie baked in a makeshift oven fashioned from a castaway Wedgewood stove's rusted firebox.

At the edge of our encampment, affixed to a prominent Douglas fir, an enameled Forest Service sign read, "Simpson Camp."

PART II

ABOUT A YEAR AND A HALF AFTER MOVING TO FOREST Glen, Zibe died. He endured his last three or four days in a tiny, private room at the hospital next door. Half a lifetime before, Eric had not returned from a tour in Vietnam, so only Eleanor was there to hold the old sheep tender's hand and usher him across to a heaven one could only hope matched his "high grass country."

Word of Zibe Simpson's passing carried me back to Simpson Camp and to preparations for our annual trips. The old sheepherder was the craftsman my father was not. In his little workshop behind their house across the creek, we once built a sailboat out of a flat, white pine board, a dowel and a red bandana. He named it the *Ellie*. "Always name a beautiful ship after a beautiful woman, little man," Zibe said, using a thick Marks-a-Lot felt pen to neatly ink her name on the bow. He carved an indentation in the bottom of the plank with a chisel and mallet. "Trap an air bubble under the boat and it'll provide buoyancy. Theoretically." Then he translated for me: "Makes 'er float."

The stale Dutch Masters stained his breath.

Weeks later, I put the *Ellie* in the pool at the willow spring adjacent to camp. It immediately nosed into the water and capsized.

"Well, *shee*-it," he said with a laugh, clasping my shoulder, "It seemed like a good idea, now didn't it, little man?"

He reached in and rescued the bandana.

~~~

"I know he hadn't much liked living in this place," Eleanor said as we sat in her quiet Forest Glen apartment. "We had such good times, more than we probably deserved, but I was getting to where I couldn't cook and he couldn't keep the weeds down. I was afraid someday the whole place—orchard, house and garden—would burn up with us inside." She smiled, and the rims of her blue eyes glistened. "Still, I think he just made do here. He just itched to be somewhere else. Anywhere else. He'd take off now and again. Get in that cute little car of mine and just drive. Only got worried one time when he came back late, all scratched up and covered with mud and crap." She blushed. "Such language. I'm sorry. Anyway, he looked pretty sheepish because he knew I'd been affright. Damned old man pushin' 90 years out there drivin' around in the dark with only one good eye. I must admit I thundered at him quite a bit."

She sipped from a teacup and thumbed through an album as I sat next to her on a tired divan from the house that didn't burn up. Occasionally, I glanced out the window at Sawmill Peak or the forestlands and thought of the pines, firs and sweeping glades of the high Coast Range.

"No, I don't seem to have any pictures of Simpson Camp. I must have thrown them all away. I mean with Zibe gone, and Eric . . ." Her voice trailed off. "He never really did go anywhere after that one time. Not even to the Builders Supply. Just took me wherever if I asked him. Doctor appointments. The store. But that was about it."

"He was a good man."

"He was a *good* man, he was."

~~~~~

I contacted the district ranger.

"Can't tell you where it is precisely," she said.

Looking at the Mendocino National Forest map, it appeared that Simpson Camp never existed. Erased. Perhaps I'd imagined the place like my own personal Brigadoon.

"I think the Washington Office is concerned about antiquities, you know, folks finding place names and going there to dig out artifacts and stuff. Add that to monitoring timber harvest and keeping the pot growers at bay." I picked up a groan from the other end of the line. The woman had given similar speeches before. "Simplest way to keep folks from rooting around old place names was to remove the place names, don't you think?"

"I suppose, and I appreciate the effort to preserve, but I just want to go for a visit. You know, to reminisce. Kinda check it out again."

"You used to work that land?"

Forty years had passed since those summer evenings by the fire.

"I knew an old man who ran sheep up that way," I said. "Used to take us up there once a year or so."

"Well, I'm not entirely sure about your camp. What was it called? Simpson?" she said, "But from what you're telling me, it might be southeast of the headwaters of the Eel, below the Yolla Bollys. In section 17, west of Smith Camp. It's somewhere in that vicinity. Probably no marker left."

A few of the place names resonated.

"You might likely be there and not know it. Like I said, the forest supervisor had those signs removed before I came on board here. Happened in some places. Other places it didn't." She closed with good luck and post-scripted: "If you know of any history about the area, I'm sure our resident archaeologist would be delighted if you could share."

~~~~

It would be a half day's trip to Zibe's old stompin' grounds, if I could find them. Into my Jeep I tossed my map case, a canteen of water and my possible sack with its length of nylon cord, bandana, small spiral notebook and pen, snakebite kit that I didn't know how to use, matches and harmonica. Before cinching the bag closed, I tossed in a couple of granola bars. I'd be home by dinner.

Halfway up Grindstone Canyon, the pavement ended. Graded gravel covered some stretches. Others were worn, chattery washboard. Twisting and climbing, a glance in the Jeep CJ's mirror displayed the Great Central Valley expanding to the east, all the way over to the foothills of the Cascades, but focus on the road was essential. I gripped the steering wheel, cringing at the thought of missing a turn, careening off into the Grindstone and becoming buzzard fodder.

Ascending out of the canyon, the route entered tall stands of conifer forest along rolling ridge tops. Snowmelt runoff seeped over the road in the highest reaches, taking with it the gravel base laid down annually to maintain the graded surface. Logging roads and skid trails split off to the left and right. Junctions that used to be labeled with an upright two-by-four hammered into the ground bearing a series of routed numbers and letters now seemed unmarked. I rattled past several, thinking that each one probably led to Simpson Camp, until the next one came along.

I folded the Mendocino National Forest map and tucked it into the crease between the bottom and back cushions of the Jeep's passenger seat. Area roads and trails, peaks and drainages were named or numbered, but the scale rendered it nearly useless. When I arrived at Mendocino Pass, I replaced the forest map with the appropriate USGS quadrangle. The quad illustrated topography and roads but didn't necessarily list everything by name. I did, however, discover that a nearby section of township and range was numbered 17.

I backtracked from the pass, assessing side roads. At one junction I noticed a one-by-two pine stake with an orange ribbon tied to the top was driven into the ground.

Twenty-first century street signs, Forest Service–style.

I crept the Jeep up a small embankment, then negotiated a tight left turn. Tires broke traction, then grabbed. Bouncing forward, the Jeep's tires settled into a pair of ruts that led through a narrow passage of wind-bent oaks, stiff, spiny manzanita and stunted yellow pines. Brittle ends of dried branches sang as they scratched both sides of the CJ. Several hundred yards west-northwest was another junction. One road followed the margin of a clearing. The other curled into a stand of firs. I chose to skirt the clearing for several hundred yards until my gut told me I was wrong.

Simpson Camp was so easy to find when Zibe or Dad was driving.

Doubling back, I saw that my tire tracks in the mottled dust established that I was the first traveler out here since the last rain, whenever that had been.

I parked at the junction and climbed out. A midday breeze slipped across my sweaty back. Like a thousand clearings in

> "Echoes of the old sheepherder's stories coursed through my head."

this high country, everything looked familiar. Even with the map, I feared being lost.

I wandered up a game trail that sliced through a verdant glade thick with grasses and wildflowers, hoping a few degrees in changed perspective might help. Cresting the ridge, a distant view of the main forest road winding toward the pass lay before me. I took in the panorama that stretched all the way out to the coast. Past midday and wishing I'd tossed in a sleeping bag and a bit more food, I came across a felled tree, its flaked bark moldering into the meadow floor. Sitting and facing west, I opened a granola bar. Before I headed home, I could at least enjoy this vista: ridge upon fading ridge, pines and glades and stream courses and, eventually, redwood groves all melting into a distant Pacific fog.

I closed my eyes. Echoes of the old sheepherder's stories coursed through my head along with pictures of the flock grazing in the high meadow. The warm afternoon sun. The freshness of the air. The soft chorus of the flock's calls. The reverie.

A sharp upslope gust slapped me to consciousness. The sun had arced closer to the sea. Amid lengthening shadows and into an increasingly insistent breeze, I headed back toward the Jeep.

Jovanna, resting

Within sight of the CJ, a low shaft of sunlight caught the flag at the top of a stake. The tiny plastic banner flapped with each breath of wind; its picket driven into the ground beside a cluster of Mule's Ear. Mule's Ear, with its thick silvery green leaves, I recalled reading somewhere, flourishes in areas often overgrazed by cattle or sheep. I remembered Jovanna lounging across the mattress she'd fashioned by knocking down a few stalks one warm mid-afternoon.

Next to the marker, ruts, magnified by erosion but partially blanketed with thick meadow foliage, coursed down the large glade. Ranging from where I stood, the clearing dipped about a half-mile to the bottom of the swale and another half mile on into the forest of firs growing on a north-facing slope.

Gathering Sticks for a Fire

I started down the hill, gingerly stepping across the scar in the meadow. Pebbles rolled from under my boots. I worried about turning an ankle in a place folks don't visit for decades at a time—or at least since the last rain. I turned to look at the Jeep parked near the top the ridge and assessed the effort necessary for me to reverse my little fool's errand. It would be a steep climb out.

The ranger's statement ran through my head repeatedly. *The Service ordered the signs down.* I could walk into and out of Simpson Camp and never know it. I looked again at the Jeep. Beyond, a shimmering sun sat mere inches atop the ridge. I wished I'd brought more granola bars and thought of the big cat that Zibe said caused them to be down one the next morning.

I headed for a tangled willow thicket that thrived on the lowest slope of the swale. Burbling from beneath, a tiny rill eclipsed the rim of a small pool. A few yards forward stood a cluster of tall, black-barked fir. I remembered Zibe's wet bandana, the one rescued from the *Ellie*, and sized up the nearby grove in the early twilight.

"If Simpson Camp is anywhere, it's here," I said aloud, knowing there could be no other soul in section 17 to make note of my declaration.

The little grove of firs looked somehow lived in. Scars in several trees' bark remained where a fence wire or corral board might have once been attached. A bent and rusted 20-penny nail pierced the blackened bark of a big fir. Ancient sap sealed the wound. Camp rags and towels had hung there,

I was sure. And one morning, tied to that nail, was the end of a taut nylon clothesline where the adults had hung my peed-in sleeping bag inside out. I fingered the ancient spike.

Serves you right for usin' that stick and playin' with the fire coals 'fore goin' to bed last night, little man, Zibe had said. *Happens ever' time. Shee . . .*

An old flush of humiliation returned that I felt in my burning cheeks.

But 40 years of forest evolution began to dissolve as a few more little recollections filtered in. Two pines standing about eight feet apart had matured since a hammock drooped between them when they were little more than saplings. The frame of the old Wedgewood firebox, once Ellie's makeshift oven, lay rusted, nearly one with the duff. Nearby, partially covered by twigs, needles and downed branches, a few blackened rocks formed a circle. In that instant, I was again 11 or 12, stumbling from the fire ring under a canopy of branches and stars after moonset, searching for my bedroll. I looked upward, imaging how the stars might peek through the tangle of fir branches now.

Forest litter covered something, and again I stumbled, jarring a curious object, long and covered by a scant layer of needles. I worked the layer of needles and duff with the toe of my boot, then with a bare hand. An aluminum ladder with the beginnings of a dusty coat of oxidation extended 10 or 12 feet. I lifted it from where the 90-year-old man had simply let it drop. Shaking off the thin layer of duff, I read: "Property of Forest Glen Senior Residences."

I scanned the nearest tree, a black-barked sentinel of the grove, then propped the ladder against the trunk of the fir. Without warning, a jolt gripped my heart, and something in my head was torn away from the present. It was as if history was dragging me back in time to a time before my childhood. A couple of feet above where the ladder now stood, well out of my reach or the reach of anyone with the US Forest Service was lag-screwed—not simply nailed—a yellowed, hand-chiseled sign with Marks-a-Lot felt pen letters: "Simpson Camp—circa 1887."

In that moment, as my head felt light and faint and disoriented, from above, a conifer whispered, "little man," while a soft, comforting hand clasped my shoulder.

Leaving the ladder standing against the tree, I began gathering sticks for a fire.

Felling the Yule Tree 2009

THE OLD GENTLEMAN COULD BE SEEN STRUGGLING to shuffle up a winter's icy hillside. Mud was beginning to cake his soft-soled shoes, and his cane had a nasty dollop on the tip as well. We younger people had hiked ahead, scouting through the grove of pine and fir for the perfect holiday tree. Occasionally, we tossed a glance over our shoulders just to see that the old man was still there. When the quest for the tree became more intense, the little check-in glances occurred less frequently, and, once over a crest, became meaningless.

A small but handsome tree was felled, but upon return, the old gent was nowhere to be seen along the muddy path. We looked at each other as our hearts sank simultaneously.

Rolling our quarry to the side of the path, one of us said, "Maybe he just wandered up an aisle."

The other: "Maybe he's just hidden by the trees."

The first: "You head over that way. I'll take this side."

"He can't be far. He's so . . ."

Some words aren't to be spoken.

Our holiday crisis was averted when, near the Christmas tree farm sales office, Papa was seen alternately warming his back side, then his front side from the glow of a huge bonfire. Facing away from the fire, he gazed at the glazed winter peaks some 30 miles east, marveling, perhaps, at their purity. When turned about, the dancing flames enchanted him. He laughed with some children, none of whom he knew, as they darted in and about; he even held one's Styrofoam cup of hot chocolate and marshmallows as the tad frolicked.

After loading up the tree, we shuffled Papa toward the truck and helped him climb in.

Once inside, the delight of the fire still glowed in his eyes. "I've been 85 years," he said, "and always had a Christmas tree in the house," he paused, "But this is the first time I ever went in the woods and actually cut one."

Then he added: "I think I'll remember this forever."

And I believe he did.

Mom's Holiday Rolls 2011

THE HANDSOME HEAP OF AROMATIC DELIGHTS—Mom's potato rolls—sat near the main course in a plastic wicker basket wrapped in a tea towel—which on any other occasion would be referred to simply as a dish cloth—and passed round the table followed by a stick of real butter placed on a saucer.

Dad grabbed a roll with one hand and sliced off an extra thick pat of butter with the other. Deftly dividing the bread along its natural creases, he'd sweep the buttery end of his Royal Danish table knife—our special occasion silverware—across one piece, then pop it in his mouth. As the now warmed butter began to slip off the silver's blade, he'd pivot another section of the roll under the butter like Willie Mays basket catching a fly ball and, again, pop the savory little morsel into his mouth. Left, then, would be the final third of a roll and a naked butter knife—affording just cause for him to cut off another chunk of butter, using a tad of it on the tidbit remains of the first sample and, seconds later, reach across the holiday board for a second potato roll.

> **"The butter and the roll will never come out even. It's a fact of life."**

"Boys," he would frequently intone to Beebo and me as he did this, "When you grow up, I think you'll discover that no matter what you do, the butter and the roll will never come out even." Then he'd add, "It's a fact of life."

This was among Dad's great truisms and one he voiced many a time when he was devouring some of Mom's homemade potato rolls during fancy dinners. Mom's creations were scratch-baked little gems formed by stuffing three tablespoon-sized wads of dough into each cup of a standard muffin tin. Out of the oven they'd come piping hot and fragrant, the perfect complement to standing rib roast at Thanksgiving, split pea soup—also homemade—on Christmas Eve, grilled T-bone steaks on New Year's Eve or ham at Easter.

Mom had long ago perfected an exasperated gasp when hearing Dad's hackneyed advice, but we knew it was simply her way of covering up the pride that welled within her when something she created was so universally appreciated.

Such appreciation didn't happen often enough.

~~~

Mom died in October of 2017 at the age of 95, having declared that 95 was "just about enough."

My daughter had copied the recipe, packed up the ingredients—bringing them 150 arduous-with-kids-miles from

Grandma's Holiday Rolls

EVER READY ROLLS

- 1 cake yeast
- 1/2 cup lukewarm water (I use the water where the potato was boiled)
- 2/3 cup shortening
- 2/3 cup sugar
- 1 teaspoon salt
- 1 cup mashed potato (I simply mash the hot potato through my strainer)
- 1 cup scalded milk
- 2 eggs, well beaten
- Flour to make stiff dough

Dissolve yeast in lukewarm water. Add shortening, sugar, salt and mashed potato to scalded milk. When cool, add yeast. Mix thoroughly and add eggs. Stir in enough flour to make stiff dough. Turn out on a slightly floured board and knead thoroughly. Put into bowl large enough to allow for slight rising, cover with cloth and set in cold part of refrigerator. About two hours before ready to serve, pinch off dough, shape and let rise until light. Bake in hot oven (400 deg. to 450) 15 to 20 minutes. Split, butter and serve hot.

Chico to Sonoma County—and baked a double batch for our Thanksgiving feast.

Mom (well, Grandma) would be so proud.

As the rolls were passed, followed by the butter, Dad's adage again held true. I, now a grandfather myself, while reaching for a second one, felt compelled to share the tidbit of my dad's wisdom with the children there assembled: "No matter what you do, the butter and the roll will never come out even. It's a fact of life."

Moments later, from somewhere—none of us quite knew where, and we all looked around—there came a familiar, exasperated gasp.

Mom, it seems, was spending a final Thanksgiving with family.

"What Is the Greatest Gift?" 2014

ROBERT HAMILTON (PAPA BOB) STEWART EMBRACED ne'er-do-wells. This I know.

My first marriage was ending. At 10:00 AM that very morning, I'd been in the Superior courtroom in Oroville being granted my dissolution of marriage's final decree. Now I was attending a church gathering at the old Boy Scout camp at Chico Meadows (northwest of Butte Meadows, California) to "entertain" congregants there by leading some songs, playing my two-dollars-from-a-junk-store Martin ukulele, telling a few jokes and doing some impressions. Evan, my commute buddy and a member of the congregation, had volunteered me to offer some campfire cheer. I flopped, I'm certain.

The Reverend Stewart, at one point either before or after the "show," cordially asked, "How ya doin'?"

Caught up in the emotions of the day, my response was something far different from simply: "Fine." I was a loser, an angry guy mad at myself—and certainly *not* an entertainer.

Apparently, someone didn't agree.

Months went by and Evan said, "You know, up at church campout, there was a lady who, well, thought you were kinda funny. She'd like to meet you."

I offered a few self-deprecating remarks, but he insisted.

A few years later, I returned to the Boy Scout camp at Chico Meadows where the Reverend Stewart officiated at the wedding of that young lady—his daughter—and me.

~~~~

After more than two decades and several moves for both Papa Bob and his wife, Pat, and for Candace and me, both of our households wound up in Placer County, California. Dinner became a weekly tradition at our home: good food, good wine, and great discussions.

I am not a churchgoer. I'd attended for a while during my first go-round at wedded bliss. But a straw broke my religious camel's back when a fellow parishioner explained his reasoning for attending our church in Chico: "It's the church where business is done." My knowledge of the Scripture was scant, but I knew the passage about Jesus and moneychangers in the temple, and I never returned.

My sanctuary became something different, something sans pews and pulpits: a filtered-light cathedral of soughing redwoods, a rocky coastal uplift serenaded by wind and gulls and crashing waves, the curves and rises of a winding secondary road accompanied by the hum and vibe of a Moto Guzzi or BMW motor. *No church pew for me, no siree.*

Still, after-dinner evenings with an 80-year-old Papa Bob caused me to recalibrate what I had come to believe about churches and Christianity. He listened. He laughed. He nodded. And he challenged. He knew the Holy Bible, but he also knew the times in which the scriptures were gathered and the reasoning behind their inclusion. His knowledge drove him to blend in his teachings of the historic church text and its current applications. *We care for the people of color* (got him kicked out of a Texas seminary—SMU—in the '40s); *we listen to grievances openly* (got him kicked out of SF State president S. I. Hiakawa's office in the '60s); *we find reason with our place and need not assume the trappings of something greater* (got him kicked out of Jim Jones's manse in the '70s). *We minister to the dispossessed* (marrying me to his only daughter).

Time advanced. In 2006, a particularly cruel cancer took his wife. Six years later, a variant set in on him. With Papa Bob no longer living independently, our weekly dinners became a bit less frequent but were always a treasure. No matter how great the pain, there were countless words of wisdom and perspective, laughter and joy.

Six weeks prior to his passing in early November, he'd somehow lost his hearing aids. We weren't sure whether they'd gotten tangled in his bedsheets or fallen on the floor to be vacuumed up by personnel at the home. In any event, he was deaf. I'd found a new recipe for Cajun salmon and sautéed some while Candi drove over to the home to pick him up.

Although, he'd not been eating of late, he downed the tidbit offered, and then reached across to the platter. He worked through the better part of two servings, washing it down with more than a few small sips of Sauvignon Blanc. His eyes shared his satisfaction with our little repast while communicating sadness for the circumstance. The inability to hear ebbed his spirit. We were reduced to either speaking uncomfortably loudly—he could pick out a little of what was said—or writing things on notes.

As the conversation waned, one of us thought of Paul's letter to the people of Corinth and wrote, "Papa Bob: What is the greatest gift?"

His eyes darted from the paper to me, to his daughter and back to me. That nearly irrepressible smile creased his tired face. He took up the pencil and simply wrote:

Postscript 1954

THE '54 FORD RANCHWAGON WAS BRAND-NEW. NOT that I remember. Dad had banged up a '46 Chevy in a collision at an intersection—a collision that, to his dying day, Mom would not let him forget—so we needed a new car. All this I was told. I was also told that in celebration of this new family car, our first road trip would be to Yosemite. In later years, Mom always boasted about packing our succession of station wagons such that no cargo rested above the lowest portion of the windows. "Safest to drive if you can see out the back," she'd said. Also safest to have a two-door car rather than a four-door car because, so she explained, when she was growing up in Houston in the '30s, some poor kid fell out the backdoor of a four-door Hudson or a Plymouth or something, landed on his head on the pavement and ". . . was probably addled for the rest of his life."

I wasn't yet three, so I don't remember anything about this first-trip-for-me to Yosemite or how the car might have been packed. I know only what I was told. And only what I was told after once, as a teenager, I happened across a yellowing Kodachrome slide shot by Dad with his trusty Signet 35.

~~~~~

The ride from LA's Altadena suburb to the valley floor must have been hours long. And, in the days before car seats or seat belts—*how ever did we survive?*—I had a lot of time to rumble around in the back seat with Beebo. I wasn't much interested in the scenery, I suppose. And even if we did have that travel bingo game—the tagboard gameboard with the little plastic windows—I would more than likely have occupied myself chewing on the gameboard's corner than matching what was outside with what was illustrated on the card.

Upon our arrival in Yosemite Valley, Dad pulled into a lovely spot in a valley floor campground backed by the river. Once the seat in front of me was unoccupied, I could easily push the seatback forward and tumble out through the open passenger door. The rushing water of a snowmelt-flushed Merced River must have been quite inviting because within moments, I was "bobbing up and down like a little redheaded cork," according to Dad, who always chuckled when he told this, "as the river sorta carried you away."

~~~~~

The old Kodachrome slide depicts me standing on a Park Service picnic table in a soaking wet didee half hanging from my little hiney. Also soaking wet is Mom's gray skirt,

Postscript 217

Mom, Beebo, Me and the Merced River

red leather shoes and white bobby socks. She is standing at the table, having just released a grasp on her shivering younger son.

The Merced River slips by in the background.

Brother Beebo looks on.

~~~

Fate—and perhaps life itself—is nothing if not fickle. Back in '54, someone—Mom—pulled me from a roiling and icy Merced River. A few years later, near our new home in Northern California, Charlie Deaver, a kid who would be about my age, was throwing sticks to his dog Rex. Charlie fell into a full-flowing Chico Creek right in front of our house.

No one was there to rescue him.

Little Charlie would never swing from that old Firestone tire slung over a sycamore branch. He would never engage in horseapple battles with the gang of neighborhood miscreants. He wouldn't hide out in Nilley's bomb shelter or memorize Bible verses for Gramma Carah or ride a motorbike into a muddy lakebed or fall in love with Rebecca Langworthy.

Those were experiences Charlie was never to have.

~~~

I know Dad wanted to get the hell out of Altadena and Southern California, and I know he simply stumbled onto the five creek-side acres with the old farmhouse. Along with that piece of real estate came bicycle racing in the back forty and paths through poison oak to swimming holes with crawdads; the squawking of pheasants on the wing, and the banditry of racoons in our trash; endless summers days and deep, starry nights. And a community of kids with parents who probably stumbled into this little stretch of paradise about the same way my folks did.

Eden it was. Eden indeed.

Charlie Deaver? I'm sorry you missed all of this. We'd have had a ball growing up together, I'm sure.

Acknowledgments

THE STORIES IN THIS COLLECTION ARE BASED UPON fuzzy recollections of real events. Some of the tales have been embellished. Some, sadly, have not. The names of many have been changed to, as one might suspect, "protect the innocent."

Unless otherwise credited, the accompanying photos are those of the author or his family.

My deepest thanks and regard to the members of the Cloverdale (California) Arts writing consortium, Annie, Jenness, Kate, Mona, Raine, Talese and others. Only through your keen eyes, kind words and a bounty of encouragement was the fulfillment of this collection possible.

To Janet Vale, coordinator—but more than that: heartbeat—of our writers' group: thanks for your editorial prowess, your insightful comments on my work and the work of others in the group and for sharing your growing-up stories with us. Beyond all that, thanks for checking in when I needed it.

To Roy Parvin, heralded, prize-winning author of short fiction and a man who should be equally noted as a teacher of both craft and the writer's experience, thanks for your patience, counsel, insight and wisdom.

To that group, know that your contributions of perspective and critical thought—if somehow unheeded—were passed over at my own risk.

Special appreciation goes to Andi Reese Brady and the team at Personal History Productions LLC for both the patience and professionalism rendered throughout the final stages of this project. The editing and design work provided by PHP helped considerably in delivering an end product that makes me look more learned, erudite and cultured than I actually *are*. Do check 'em out at www.personalhistoryproductions.com. Perhaps your review of their services will prompt you to write down and share your own stories with loved ones.

~~~

To the neighborhood kids—and their parents—each of whom were characters in the adventures and misadventures of my growing up, know that these stories could not have happened without you. We were given the best of childhoods, hands down.

I'll never be certain if Mom and Dad fully appreciated the gift they gave to Beebo and me when they uprooted their little family from a tidy and comfortable Southern California

Acknowledgments 221

Mom, Beebo and Me: "Lunch is on us, Mom."

post-war home and moved to a ramshackle fixer-upper on five acres facing a creek.

I am certain that neither of us ever really said thanks.

This little volume will have to suffice.

About the Author

IN 1957, DAVE DELGARDO'S FATHER MADE SURE THAT his family escaped the congestion and smog of the Los Angeles basin, moving 500 miles north to Chico, California. A far cry from the city, David's growing-up years were spent on a five-acre parcel of almond and fruit trees facing a creek where he and his gang of friends built tree forts and bonfires and caught crawdads and poison oak.

Author self-portrait, age 6

A 35-year career in public education found Delgardo moving from assignments throughout Northern California, from the Gold Country and the Sierra to the Wine Country and the Redwoods. Retired, with his wife Candace, he spends much of his time exploring California and the West on two wheels or four, always looking for the next great place.

But wherever he lives or wherever he travels, recollections of small town Chico always call him home.

www.ingramcontent.com/pod-product-compliance
Lightning Source LLC
Chambersburg PA
CBHW030323100526
44592CB00010B/542